Esteban Echeverría

Courtesy Museo Nacional de Bellas Artes Buenos Aires

ESTEBAN ECHEVERRÍA

ESTEBAN ECHEVERRÍA

By
Edgar C. Knowlton, Jr.

University of Hawaii

For Professor and Mrs. A. S. Cook in souvenir of the Stanford Mallarmé Festival — with aloha, Edgar C Knowlton J. XI. 96

DORRANCE & COMPANY, INCORPORATED
828 LANCASTER AVENUE • BRYN MAWR, PENNSYLVANIA 19010
Publishers Since 1920

— For Spanish Studies Albert Cook

To the memory of my mother, Mildred M. (Hunt) Knowlton, and of my first Spanish teacher at Middlebury, Concha Bretón, to her friend and colleague, Justina Ruiz de Conde, to Aurelio M. Espinosa, Jr., who guided me in the study of Spanish both at Harvard and at Stanford, to those who introduced me to the study of Spanish-American literature at Stanford: Ronald Hilton and Juan B. Rael, and to Stephen C. Ventura and his family, who have encouraged me to continue my work and studies.

Contents

About the Author

Edgar C. Knowlton, Jr., Professor of European Languages at the University of Hawaii at Manoa, obtained his degrees from Harvard and from Stanford, having served as teaching fellow or assistant at both universities. He also studied at the Middlebury College Spanish and Italian summer schools and one summer at the Universidad Autónoma, Guadalajara, in Mexico. Besides teaching (and studying) at the University of Hawaii, he taught under United States State Department grants as Visiting Professor of Linguistics at the University of Malaya in Kuala Lumpur and at the Universidad Central de Venezuela in Caracas. He coauthored with A. Grove Day for Twayne the volume on V. Blasco Ibáñez, and his translation from Portuguese of Sá de Meneses's epic, *Malaca conquistada,* published in 1971 by the University of Malaya Press, won the Translation Prize from the Secretaria de Estado de Informação e Turismo in Lisbon in 1973. He has published articles on Esteban Echeverría, subject of this study, in *Hispania* and in the *Boletín de la Academia Argentina de Letras.* In 1973 he worked on Echeverría in libraries in Buenos Aires and in Montevideo. Travel has taken him to most New World Spanish-speaking countries as well as to Spain, the Philippines, Portugal, Brazil, France, and England. He has lectured at universities in Berlin, Korea, Malaysia, the Philippines, at the Sociedade de Geografia in Lisbon, and participated in international congresses in Arequipa, Caracas, Kuala Lumpur, Manila, Maringá, Mexico City, and Tokyo.

Preface

Esteban Echeverría's life is one of the most inspiring in the history of Spanish America; its four and a half decades closely coincide with the independence years and the development of individual nations. Travel to France, England, and Brazil broadened his horizons and brought him in contact, in early manhood, with political and social liberal ideas, as well as with the great masters of European literary Romanticism.

Admiration of Lord Byron as man and poet led him to seek to become a New World Byron; his adult life was marked by chronic and life-threatening illness, which lends an eternal appeal to his introspective lyrics. Poverty and exile were his reward for his vigorous fight against the despotic regime of the notorious strong man of Argentina, Juan Manuel de Rosas.

Echeverría made himself a writer of distinction in part through will power; he felt his command of Spanish was not equal to his goal in emulating Lord Byron, and part of his stay in Paris was devoted to painstaking study of masters of the Spanish language. There can be no doubt that Echeverría recognized that he could assume the role of mentor to the young intellectuals of the 1830s in Buenos Aires, and that establishing a reputation as poet was an essential part of the mission.

Neoclassical, European models were in vogue; it is largely due to Echeverría that the freshness of Romanticism's political and literary freedoms was effectively implanted in the River Plate countries. That this was possible is doubtless because of Echeverría's desire to Americanize Europe's Romanticism, that is, to create in his native land works equivalent to those of Europe of that time, but works with a New World, relevant setting.

A constant theme, which makes his work timely even today, is the attack on dictatorship. Eras come and go, but the conflict between authoritarianism and liberalism has continued to be a vital part of Spanish America. Another theme is that of the development of a viable nation from a colonial past, one which has assumed a renewed importance in recent years, in literature as well as in political matters.

Readers of this study of Echeverría will, it is presumed, have a primary interest in his works. There is an autobiographical tone to his writing, partly the result of the interest of the Romantic in individuality, and partly stemming from his concern with the actuality of his day. Echeverría was a literary critic in spirit, and had the belief that literature should idealize rather than copy life; this means that it is sometimes difficult for a modern reader to know how to interpret some of his work. The fact that his greatest masterpiece was published about twenty years after his death means that this work has excited a perplexing variety of interpretation.

The best course seems to be to indicate the most important views, point out clues given by Echeverría in his own writing, and not impose single views, however tempting.

A small portion of Echeverría's work is available in English; therefore, it seems wise to cite more passages in the original than might otherwise be the case. There are excellent studies of Echeverría, his life and works, but almost all of them are in Spanish and take for granted knowledge that to non-Spanish American readers may be uncommon. This accounts for the presentation sometimes of elementary facts for the benefit of North American readers that would be out of place for the specialists or compatriots of Echeverría.

Gutiérrez, Echeverría's friend, is still the prime source for biography and for the edition of the works; in the fifth volume of his edition are two sets of pages with Roman numerals. The second consists of "Critical Judgments;" in this case, the key words, "Juicios críticos" have been used. In quoting reproduction of the text as exactly as possible, save obvious errors, has been the goal. Current usage for accents and spelling has been followed.

Echeverría made interesting use of epigraphs, tags from his favorite writers that often give concisely the themes and motifs of his work. In the hope that identification of the sources of the epigraphs might be illuminating for students of general literature, an attempt has been made to be specific in this regard.

To sum up, it would be hard to improve upon the assessment made of Echeverría's contribution to Spanish-American literature by the distinguished turn of the century Uruguayan essayist, José Enrique Rodó, who referred to Echeverría, "con quien llegó, del otro lado de los mares, el fuego de la gran revolución ideal que embellece y exalta las primeras décadas del pasado siglo; y levantaba, como una triple afirmación del porvenir, una idea de emancipación literaria, un propósito de regeneración social y una norma de organización política." (Rodó, *Obras completas,* Madrid: Aguilar, 1957, p. 675) ("with whom there arrived, from across the seas, the fire of the great revolution of ideas that beautifies and exalts the first decades of the last century; and raised, as a triple affirmation of the future, an idea of literary emancipation, a purpose of social regeneration and a norm of political organization.")

Acknowledgments

The author wishes to acknowledge his debt to Samuel F. Oliver, Director General of Museums and Libraries, the National Museum of Fine Arts of Buenos Aires for a copy of Carlos Pellegrini's pencil and watercolor portrait of the poet done in 1831, and for permission for its use as frontispiece in this volume; to José E. Vargas, Chief, Technical Unit of Cultural Policies and Finance, Organization of American States, for permission to quote passages cited from: Domingo Faustino Sarmiento, *Travels; A Selection*. Trans. by Inés Muñoz. Washington, D.C., Organization of American States, 1963; to Donald W. Bleznick, Editor of *Hispania,* for permission to make use of material included in his article, "The Epigraphs in Esteban Echeverría's 'La Cautiva,'" in that journal, 44 (1961): 212–217; to the late Roberto F. Giusti for his generosity in answering questions by correspondence and for hospitality extended to the author in Martínez in 1973; to Raúl M. Castagnino of the Academia Argentina de Letras in Buenos Aires for similar generosity; to William O. Cord, former Editor, Latin American Series, Twayne Publishers, Inc., and to A. Grove Day, one-time collaborator and friend, for advice in making changes from an earlier form of this study; to Doris M. Ladd and Ştefan Baciu, colleagues and mentors in Latin American history and literature, respectively, for special guidance in their fields; to Alfredo Lepro, Ambassador of Uruguay in Portugal in 1973, for an interest manifested by gifts of relevant books and suggestions for the research; to the various libraries in Buenos Aires and Montevideo where the author was accorded help and cooperation; and to his mother, Mildred M. Knowlton, an inspiring, patient, and hard-working helper in the Echeverría quest. Kitty and Michael W. Dabney helped at a crucial time with expert typing and advice.

Chronology

1805—José Esteban Antonino Echeverría born September 2 in Buenos Aires. His parents were José Domingo Echeverría, a Basque from Spain, and Martina Espinosa of Buenos Aires.

1816—Death of the poet's father; he enters the San Telmo school.

1822—Death of the poet's mother; he continues his studies.

1823—Leaves school for the employ of the Messrs. Sebastián Lezica and Brothers; studies French.

1825—Leaves the company; sets sail for France via Bahia and Pernambuco.

1826—Lands at Le Havre; reaches Paris; embarks on studies there.

1829—Spends a month or more in London.

1830—Leaves Le Havre for Buenos Aires; stops at Montevideo en route.

1832—November. Leaves for Mercedes, on the Río Negro, in Uruguay in a futile effort to improve his health.

1833—May. Returns to Buenos Aires.

1834—Publishes *Los consuelos (The Consolations)*; wins esteem.

1837—June 23. Formation of the Literary Salon; he takes part.

1837—Publication of *Rimas (Rhymes)*, including "La cautiva" ("The Captive Woman").

1838—May. Closing of the Literary Salon; June. Organization of the Association of May.

1838—July 8 or 9. Birth of the Association of the Young Generation of Argentina, a secret society, for which he writes the Credo.

1838—December. Goes to Los Talas, country estate of his brother.

1839—February 15. Publication of the Credo, anonymously, in the Montevideo newspaper, *El Iniciador*.

1839—October and November. The insurrection of the South takes place.

1840—August/September. Lavalle fails in his attempt to overthrow the Rosas dictatorship; Echeverría goes into exile, reaching La Colonia del Sacramento, Uruguay.

1841—June. Leaves La Colonia del Sacramento for Montevideo.

1844—May and June. In polemic with José Rivera Indarte, editor of *El Nacional*.

1846—Publication of the *Dogma socialista (Socialist Dogma)*, a revision of the earlier Credo; also publishes the *Manual de enseñanza moral (Manual of Moral Instruction)*.

1847—Publication of the *Cartas a D. Pedro de Angelis (Letters to Don Pedro de Angelis)*.

1848—Revolution in France, which causes Echeverría to prepare a commentary, published in the same year.

1849—Publication of *Insurrección del Sur (Insurrection of the South)* and of *La Guitarra (The Guitar)*.

1850—Publication of *Avellaneda*.

1851—January 19. Death in Montevideo; a daughter, Martina, survives him.

1870–1874—Publication of *Obras Completas (Complete Works)*, annotated by Echeverría's friend, Juan María Gutiérrez. A number of these publications never appeared in Echeverría's lifetime.

CHAPTER 1

GEOGRAPHICAL AND HISTORICAL SETTING

I. A Bit of Geography

Without a feeling for geography (including population and climate) the American reader is apt to be misled in reading Echeverría's works, since they are often tied very closely to their River Plate setting.

The seasons are reversed in the southern hemisphere; most Americans know this as a fact, but still there is a strong temptation to think of May as May (instead of being similar to November in the other hemisphere), or of snow at Christmastime.

Professor Amado Alonso, who taught and lived in Buenos Aires before beginning his Harvard career in 1946, made a deep impression when he stated that the natives of Buenos Aires also enjoyed a white Christmas, like those of Boston and Cambridge. He went on to explain that in the case of Buenos Aires, however, the whiteness was not due to snow, but rather was the whiteness of metals under the process of being forged, when they glow with white heat. This was, clearly, an exaggeration, but it illustrated well that the climate of Buenos Aires was similar to that of New England in its variation, and that cold weather in Boston would be matched by hot weather in the same month in Buenos Aires. The hottest month in Buenos Aires is January, with a mean temperature of 24° Celsius (74° Fahrenheit) and an absolute maximum of 40° Celsius (104° Fahrenheit). The coolest there is June with a mean of 9° Celsius (49° Fahrenheit) and absolute minimum of −6° Celsius (22° Fahrenheit).

May 25, 1810 in Buenos Aires gave rise to this sort of weather: "The morning . . . dawned cold and drizzling—one of those miserable, melancholy autumnal days for which May in Buenos Aires is noted."[1] Against this background took place the confrontation between members of the cabildo or town council and the people, and again, a weather phenomenon: "Tradition has it that at the moment the people shouted their answer to the members of the cabildo the sun forced its way through a rift in the leaden clouds and shone down on the scene. This sun has become known as the *sol de Mayo,* sun of May, and appears in the center of the Argentine flag and on the coat-of-arms."[2] May plays a key role in the feeling for independence for the people of that country, and part of the connotation depends on the fact that there was something special about the sun's appearance at that moment. It is obvious that "sun of May" has a very different meaning to a native of Buenos Aires than it has—without explanation—to a North American who understands the words with reference to his own experience.

Whenever the words Buenos Aires are read today by a North American, there is a temptation to associate it with the urban, Europeanized cultural

1

center of the twentieth century. A reference to population statistics for the early nineteenth century is a desirable corrective. "In 1810 the total population of the Viceroyalty was estimated at 720,000, composed of 421,000 mestizos, 210,000 Indians, 60,000 mulattoes, 20,000 Negroes, 6,000 European whites, and 3,000 native-born whites. About 60 percent of this population was in what is today Argentina. Most of the whites and nearly all the Negroes and mulattoes were in Argentina and Uruguay, while the population of Peru and Bolivia was mostly Indian and mestizo. The population of the city of Buenos Aires at the time of the revolution was 45,500."[3] The growth in population of the city of Buenos Aires between 1797 and 1854/ 5 may be seen in the following statistics: "40,000 in 1797; 62,228 in 1836; and 90,076 in 1854/5."[4] World population was, of course, in this era much lower than at present, but a reader must not think that the Buenos Aires of Echeverría's day was similar in size to that of today.

Another source contrasts clearly the ethnic makeup of the Argentina of 1810 and that of the twentieth century: "The twenty million people of modern Argentina are mostly of Spanish and Italian extraction and constitute (with the Uruguayans) the most homogeneous white population of any nation of Latin America. There is some Indian blood in the people of the interior, especially in the piedmont area against the Andean wall; however, only twenty to thirty thousand Argentines can be accurately described as Indians."[5] A more recent population estimate gives 25,720,000 people, with 97 percent Europeans (Spanish and Italian), the rest Indians, Mestizos, and Arabs.[6] In contrast, "The population pattern of 1810, when a handful of Buenos Aires creoles took the first step toward separation from Spain, was quite different from that of the mid-twentieth century. In that year, there may have been about 400,000 people in the area now comprising Argentina; half or more of these were Indians, 20,000 Negroes, 60,000 mulattoes, many thousand mestizos, and no more than 9,000 whites. We may hazard the guess that the effective literate section of the Argentine population of 1810 was not greater than the present population of such towns as Darien, Connecticut or Grinnell, Iowa."[7]

The large Indian population reflects the fact that in 1810 the campaigns against the Indians had not yet brought them under the effective control of the Buenos Aires government. One phenomenon of population taking place in the period of Echeverría's lifetime was absorption: "From the censuses and accounts of travelers in the first decades of the nineteenth century emerges a rough average of five hundred thousand to six hundred thousand as the total population of Argentina at the time of independence. Of this figure probably 30 percent were Indian and 10 percent were Negro and mulatto. The remainder were creole and mestizo, but, at least within the urban and coastal areas, the creole had begun to absorb the mestizo. By the 1820s, therefore, the creole–mestizo stock predominated, and the darker shadings of mestizo and Indian elements became pronounced only in the countryside or in the interior. The Negro and mulatto strain was evident in the towns, accounting for more than a quarter of the population in Buenos Aires, but even mere miscegenation was gradually absorbing the Negro into the mestizo ranks."[8]

Population statistics of Montevideo, the neighboring city to Buenos Aires where Echeverría took refuge from the dictatorship of Rosas during the last ten years of his life, are provided by another Argentinian exile, Domingo Faustino Sarmiento, and serve as comparison: "In October 1843 the census showed these curious results: Inhabitants of the city: Orientales, 11,431; Americans, 3,170; Europeans, 15,252; Africans (Free), 1,344."[9] The categories may need explanation: the Orientales were natives of the Banda Oriental or East Bank, corresponding to modern Uruguay; the Americans were composed largely of South Americans, the majority being from Argentina; the Europeans included immigrants from Genoa, the Basques, the Galicians from northwestern Spain, Italians, French, Germans, English, Canary Islanders, and other Spaniards.[10]

Geographically Uruguay has much in common with the Humid Pampa of Argentina, from which it differs chiefly in having somewhat more hilly terrain than its neighbor. There are three other chief divisions in Argentina: the Andes, the north (including the Chaco and the Paraná Plateau), and Patagonia, but it is the area of the pampas which includes both humid and dry parts and extends to Buenos Aires along the River Plate that provided most of the setting for Echeverría's nationalistic works. The pampa has changed, too, in the course of the centuries, from being filled with areas of trees and *monte* vegetation, partially burned out by Indians for their hunting and war needs, to famous areas in which Argentina's cattle could graze. This region was dominated by man on horseback; there were no fences; wagons pulled by oxen could cross the pampa surface. There was a system of forts built roughly along the line of the Río Salado, within which the estancias or ranches could with comparative safety raise cattle and livestock.[11] It is this region which provides the setting for the action of Echeverría's "La cautiva" ("The Captive Woman").

II. Argentina's History up to Independence

Although earlier in the sixteenth century there were short-lived attempts to establish settlements in the part of South America where Buenos Aires is now located, along the River Plate, its character as a permanent Spanish settlement begins only in 1580 with a party which had reached there from Asunción in present-day Paraguay. Other settlements in the northwestern part of the present Argentina were made by colonists from Peru or Chile, with Lima as their viceregal capital. Córdoba was the most famous of the early settlements and for a time was both an intellectual and a religious center. In 1776 was created the Viceroyalty of the River Plate, which had Buenos Aires as its administrative center, and established a sort of unity over present-day Argentina, Paraguay, Uruguay (the East Bank), and part of Bolivia. At the end of the eighteenth century a meat-salting plant was established in Buenos Aires, a great stimulus to the economy with the production of fats and salted meat from the large cattle herds that grazed on the pampas.

After the formation of the Viceroyalty, direct trade became possible between Buenos Aires and Spain as well as Spain's other colonies, a great improvement over the earlier routing of trade through Lima. Contraband trade with England had existed when the center of trade was supposed to be at Lima, and persisted even when the port of Buenos Aires was opened for Spain and its colonies. Free trade became an issue for colonial discontent with recognition of the economic advantages of trade with countries other than the Hispanic ones, particularly with England.

In 1777 the Peace of San Ildefonso transferred the East Bank from Portuguese control; the Portuguese had been engaged in smuggling at Montevideo and at Colonia. Thus what is now Uruguay became part of the Viceroyalty of the River Plate.

There existed also dissatisfaction with the treatment given to the inhabitants of the colonies in comparison with the government representatives and employees from the homeland.

Upsetting to the prestige of Spain's viceroy in Buenos Aires was his demonstrated weakness when this official fled to avoid capture by a British fleet on June 17, 1806. General William Carr Beresford behaved well, respecting the religion of the *porteños,* as the inhabitants of Buenos Aires are called, announcing that open trade with England could begin. In about six weeks, the French-born Santiago de Liniers led a group of men against Buenos Aires, joining the inhabitants to force the British to leave.

After the surrender of Beresford and 1,200 of his men, the people of Buenos Aires met in open council or a *cabildo abierto* on August 14, 1806, an instance of self-rule that was stimulating to a desire for independence.

Meanwhile, the British organized for a second attack on Buenos Aires. They began by taking Montevideo on February 3, 1807 and the same viceroy who had fled from Beresford's forces made his escape from Montevideo, where he was in command. After the capture of Montevideo the British commander, General John Whitelocke, arrived to lead an attack on Buenos Aires. In late June, Captain Liniers and his criollo men were defeated by the British at the Riachuelo, but when the British entered the city itself they encountered such determined resistance that they surrendered in defeat; General Whitelocke promised to leave Buenos Aires immediately and also that they would subsequently withdraw from Montevideo and the East Bank or Uruguay.

People in both cities had seen the advantages of free trade, and the helplessness of Spain as represented by the viceroy; the *porteños* now forced the resignation of Spain's viceroy and elected Liniers as his successor.

King Charles IV confirmed Liniers as interim Viceroy. Meantime, because of Portugal's refusal to participate in the blockade imposed by Napoleon against the British Isles, Napoleon directed his attention toward the

4

Iberian peninsula. He decided to invade Portugal through Spain; his general entered Lisbon late in 1807. In March of 1808 Spain was invaded by French troops as part of Napoleon's campaign against the British. Charles IV abdicated in favor of his son, who later became Ferdinand VII, but both father and son were taken by Napoleon at Bayonne, and the throne of Spain was given to Napoleon's brother, Joseph. The Spaniards rose up against French rule; Joseph was proclaimed king on July 6, 1808, but left Madrid, returning only in December when Napoleon himself had taken over the Spanish campaign in person. Spain refused, however, to submit and attempted to continue its national rule through a central *junta*; Liniers was replaced by a new viceroy, Baltasar Hidalgo de Cisneros.

The rapid changes in rule in Buenos Aires had produced a bad effect on Buenos Aires's economy and trade. In an 1809 pamphlet, Mariano Moreno suggested the re-opening of the port of Buenos Aires to free trade, a move seen as useful by merchants and also by government treasury officials. The viceroy acceded; the creoles saw this as another indication of their strength, and the economic situation improved.

In May 1810 came news from Spain that only the *junta* in Cadiz was free of French control. The demand was made for an open *cabildo* or town meeting; the viceroy accepted this demand and on May 22 the first day of discussion took place. On May 25 occurred what is for the people of Argentina the birth of their independence, the decision of the *cabildo* to form a provisional *junta* for the provinces of the River Plate, to govern for Ferdinand VII of Spain, still in Napoleon's power. The viceroy and his officials were deported to the Canary Islands; included as members of the *junta* in Buenos Aires were Mariano Moreno, the author of the pamphlet of 1809, and other distinguished members of this generation, Manuel Belgrano and Bernardino Rivadavia.

These men were all inspired by the ideas of the great French Encyclopaedists of the eighteenth century, men like Rousseau and Voltaire. As slogan of the Buenos Aires uprising against the Spanish colonial order is the French call to liberty, the Phrygian cap above the clasped hands of Liberty, Equality, Fraternity, commemorated in the coat of arms of the nation.

Blue and white became the symbolic colors associated with Argentina as an independent nation.

The uprising, it should be emphasized, was brought about by pressure, and without violence; it is possible to question the sincerity of the desire to govern for Spain's Ferdinand VII, ostensibly the goal of the *junta*, on the part of a man like Mariano Moreno; in any case, the control by Spain came to its end on May 25.

More than four years were to pass during which the revolutionists of Buenos Aires sought to extend further the independence from Spain to include Bolivia, Paraguay, the East Bank (or Uruguay), which had formed part of the colonial Viceroyalty. They culminated in the signing of the Argentinian Declaration of Independence on July 9, 1816. Juan Martín de Pueyrredón became Supreme Director. Ferdinand VII of Spain had been restored to power

5

in Spain in 1814, but he never was granted the allegiance of Argentinian leaders. The effort to include Paraguay as part of the new nation was unsuccessful, as was that to secure the part of Bolivia which had formed a section of the Viceroyalty. The East Bank was, for a time, linked with Argentina under José Artigas, who was in favor of a federal system of government. This led him to seek independence from Buenos Aires' control.

Independence from royalists' control was assured by the defeats of the royalists by the forces of the new government under the command of Manuel Belgrano near Tucumán and at Salta in the northwestern part of Argentina.

In recent years historians have questioned the amount of social and economic change effected by the Latin American wars of independence, how much, for example, the life of the Indian was affected by the change of government from the peninsular Spanish colonial rulers to the new creole or mestizo leadership. In the case of Argentina, the effect was indirect; free trade was a factor in the expansion of the cattle sector of the economy; this required expansion of the grazing lands, with the resultant pushing back of the Indian frontier.

This means that the point of view with regard to national independence varies in accordance with the background of the individual; Echeverría or the *porteño* of education will almost of necessity have a very different point of view from the owner of a ranch or *estancia*, or from the *gaucho* of the pampas.

III. *Argentina from Independence to the Fall of Rosas*

In 1817 General José de San Martín undertook the campaign of the Andes, one of the most successful campaigns in military history, which was to culminate in the liberation of Peru in July, 1821. The Revolution had been extended far beyond its original scope. It was only a matter of time before General San Martín resigned, and General Simón Bolívar at Junín and General Antonio José de Sucre at Ayacucho won the final victories over Royalist Spanish forces.

Supreme Director Pueyrredón was strong, but it was not possible for him to end civil war in the provinces, each of which was governed by its own chief or *caudillo*. There was a difference in way of life and political attitudes between urban city dwellers (particularly those of the chief port and capital, Buenos Aires) and those in the rural areas, dominated by the *estanciero* or estate-owner and the *gaucho*. The *gaucho*, often a mestizo, was the frontiersman who—in the course of decades—had developed an individual and unusual lifestyle, in opposition to the Indian, but like him often living beyond the law, on the pampas. In general, those of the rural areas disliked the idea of taking orders from the élite of Buenos Aires and wished for autonomy or decentralization. Those of Buenos Aires tended to prefer the idea of a strong central government with the city as holder of political power.

This was the basic problem faced by Pueyrredón and his various successors. On April 22, 1819 a federal constitution was drawn up by the districts surrounding Buenos Aires, but the capital did not recognize it; Pueyrredón resigned on June 11, 1819.

Federalists and Unitarians are the names applied to opponents in the rapidly changing political scene of the decade that followed. Federalists favored local autonomy and held to traditional ideas about immigration, the Church, education, and the economy. The Unitarians, on the other hand, were liberal in political views, subscribed generally to the ideals of the eighteenth century French Encyclopaedists and the French revolution, and sought the existence of a progressive, centralized state centered about Buenos Aires as the capital. The *caudillos* of the various outlying states, with their *gaucho* followers, exerted effective power where they were, with little or no attention to the desires of the governments in Buenos Aires. Bernardino Rivadavia, a Unitarian, showed his capability during his period in office, but failed to win over the provinces. War with Brazil proved to be an additional problem. Artigas had been ousted by Brazilian troops and in 1821 Uruguay or the East Bank was incorporated into Brazil. In 1825 Argentina helped Uruguay in its revolt against Brazil, and on February 20, 1827 the Brazilians were defeated by the combined forces of Argentina and Uruguay. Instead of being incorporated as part of Argentina, however, Uruguay was made an independent country.

Rivadavia had the idea that Argentina should emulate the civilized countries of Europe; he felt that the power of the Church should be curtailed in the interest of progress, and that women should play a role in public affairs. He organized a beneficent society of Buenos Aires women with humanitarian goals. He tried to encourage secular education and sponsored public works to be used for growth and development. He distributed public lands under emphyteusis, whereby the nation continues to own its lands but permits use of those lands under certain arrangements. Lands could be rented for a twenty-year term with a designated rate of rent to be paid; it is a question whether Rivadavia's intentions were pragmatic or not—it is certain that the rental would provide a new source of government income—but one result was that public lands came under the control of a small group of people. Rivadavia, despite his progressiveness, failed to achieve what he had hoped for and resigned in July, 1827.

He was succeeded by Manuel Dorrego, a Federalist, also a man of ability, but in 1828 troops under General Lavalle, fresh from fighting against Brazilian forces in Uruguay, dissatisfied with terms of the peace treaty, took part in a revolt against the government; Dorrego was captured and shot. Another Federalist, Juan Manuel de Rosas, who had supported Dorrego, a powerful *caudillo*, avenged with his *gauchos* the death of Dorrego by defeating General Lavalle and forcing him into exile. In late 1829 Rosas was given the position of governor of Buenos Aires. During his three-year term he brought order and stability by means of the astute exercise of special powers given to him as Restorer of the Laws. He united the *caudillos* sym-

7

pathetic to Federalism, and defeated the others; he catered to the favor of the lower classes, particularly to the blacks, who admired him and his wife, Doña Encarnación Ezcurra. Other ranchers and the rural people thought of him as a heroic *gaucho* type. Blue and white of the revolutionary period gave way to the blood-red ribbons and uniforms under Rosas. His portrait was displayed by the members of the public who either sincerely admired him or thought it prudent to pretend to do so. When Rosas took office, the control was divided among General José María Paz, a cultivated Unitarian military man who was in control of nine provinces of the west and northwest joined as a Liga Unitaria or Unitarian League, Estanislao López in the Littoral provinces, and Rosas in the province of Buenos Aires. López joined in a pact with Rosas to destroy the Unitarians. In May, 1831, General Paz suffered capture, having been unhorsed by the famous *boleadoras* of the pampa Indians, which came to be part of the weaponry of the *gaucho*. The *boleadoras* are composed of *bolas*, or weights attached to a rope swung at the legs of cattle or game, entangling them, and causing the animal hit by them to fall down. He was turned over to Rosas who had him kept in prison for seven years.

In late 1832, Rosas refused reelection and accepted the mission of campaigning against the Indians in the south. He went south to the Río Colorado; his soldiers were able to kill some 6,000 Indians and set free a number of their captives, and the campaign was a success, opening up large areas for settlement. Matters did not go well in Buenos Aires in his absence, and Rosas was invited back to assume control, by a measure legislated in Buenos Aires on March 7, 1835, which invested him with virtually complete power and nominated him to be governor and captain-general of the province of Buenos Aires for a five-year period. Rosas asked that a plebiscite be taken. In fact, there was little opposition; a strong man seemed to be necessary to maintain order. The vote was announced as 9,315 to 5. Rosas was successful in controlling the other *caudillos* for the period between 1835 and the end of his rule in 1852, when he was forced into exile in England after his army was defeated by that of one of his fellow *caudillos*, Justo José Urquiza, of the province of Entre Ríos.

Particularly in the early years of Rosas's rule there was an active artistic and intellectual life in Buenos Aires, in which the salon of Mariquita Sánchez, wife of the Consul of France, was a gathering place. It was attended by such men as Carlos E. Pellegrini, the painter; Juan Pedro Esnaola, the musician; and Echeverría's friend and biographer, Juan María Gutiérrez.

During the period between Rosas's first three-year term and his return to power, his wife, Doña Encarnación Ezcurra, who remained in Buenos Aires, is alleged to have made efforts to discredit the administrations and to have enlisted spies to find those who were in opposition to Rosas. The group known as the *mazorca*, a word meaning "ear of corn," which symbolized unity, functioned secretly and made use of the tactics of terrorism to spread fear among the Unitarians and any other opponents of Rosas. Like many names, *mazorca* lends itself to facetious misinterpretations; its potential victims thought that its name should be spelled as two words, *más horca*, "more gallows." Since *h* is a silent letter in Spanish, and *s* and *z* are pronounced alike in most Spanish-American dialects, the pun is perfect.

In addition to the relative stability imposed by Rosas's regime, his land policy has been praised for having had a beneficial effect on the pastoral industries.[12]

Liberals could only be dismayed at Rosas's rule and tyranny. Reaction against him was steady. In 1838, Echeverría and others helped organize a liberal secret society, somewhat like the Young Italy or Young Europe of Mazzini. There were various armed revolts, one in the province of Corrientes in March, 1839, which resulted in the death of the governor of Corrientes, Berón de Astrada, and a victory for Rosas; in October and November, 1839, another one began at Dolores and was crushed at the battle of Chascomús; another was led by General Juan Lavalle, who landed at San Pedro on July 5, 1840 but was forced to withdraw at the end of August. By September and October of 1841 the continued efforts of General Lavalle and others had led to the deaths of that general and of General Marco Avellaneda.

Argentina's neighbor Uruguay became involved in a civil war between the Colorados or Reds, led by Fructuoso Rivera, president of Uruguay from 1830 to 1835, and the Blancos or Whites, led by Manuel Oribe, Rivera's successor, forced to resign because of the Colorados' revolt in 1838. Oribe fled to Argentina, and was supported by Rosas, and a siege of Montevideo began, lasting more than nine years. The intervention of Argentina in the civil war in Uruguay caused trouble with France and with England. This led to the closing of the Paraná river to foreign trade, and a blockade of the River Plate by naval forces of those two countries.

The blockade was lifted in 1847–1848, a moral victory for Rosas against the European powers, but the policy of Rosas to favor Buenos Aires economically over other provinces was a source of irritation, and his fellow *caudillo* in Entre Ríos, Urquiza, made an agreement with Rosas's enemies, the governments of Brazil and of Uruguay, after which he went to relieve the besieged city of Montevideo. This took place in 1851, and in the next year Urquiza's troops defeated those of Rosas at Monte Caseros. He and his daughter, Manuelita, took flight and went into exile in England.

CHAPTER 2

ECHEVERRÍA, MAN AND LEGEND

In the case of Echeverría, the history and geography of Argentina form part of the literary work and are basic to the understanding of the man. A knowledge of his temperament, character, and changes of fortune is fundamental to an appreciation of his multifaceted work. Part of this is due to his role as a pioneer, as a teacher to the youth of Argentina. The introduction of Romanticism to Argentina, a source of the respected Constitution of Argentina, the first masterpiece of prose narration in an independent Hispanic America, at least partial responsibility for the overthrow of the dictator Rosas—all these have been credited to Echeverría. The work often permits insights into the character of the man, but to consider the work without reference to Echeverría's life or to his reputation and the legend that became connected with him would be to come to a very partial assessment of his achievement as a writer.

Students of Echeverría are fortunate in having available a sympathetic, beautifully expressed biography, prepared by his friend and contemporary, Juan María Gutiérrez. This sketch of Echeverría's life is part of both editions of the complete works of the poet, but is not available in English translation. Such a translation would have value and interest, but for the present it must be sufficient to make use of the information and judgments provided in it, together with the additions and rectifications of detail made by later students of Echeverría's life, to prepare an account of his life for readers of this volume which would emphasize aspects of direct relevance to the appreciation of his writings.

During this chapter and the remaining chapters, references to material found in the 1870–1874 edition by Juan María Gutiérrez of the complete works of Echeverría will be made, as appropriate, by reference in the text within parentheses, followed by volume number (there are five volumes) and page number, whether or not the reference is to one of Echeverría's works or to a section, e.g. the account of his life by the editor, which was authored by someone other than the poet. Bibliographical details regarding the edition are found in our Bibliography.

I. The Early Years

José Esteban Antonino Echeverría was born on September 2, 1805 in the *barrio* popularly known as *del alto*, "of the height," to Don José Domingo Echeverría, a native of the Spanish province of Biscay, a businessman, and Doña Martina Espinosa, a native of Buenos Aires. The expression *del alto* is an abbreviation of del Alto de San Pedro, "of St. Peter's Height," height in opposition to the low sections near the banks of the River Plate, which took its name from the high church of San Pedro Telmo, patron saint of navigators. Echeverría was the third of nine children.[1] The general atmosphere of Echeverría's birthplace has been described as a *barrio* of young men willing to settle their differences with dagger-thrusts, abundant in taverns, lying between the river and the pampa, inhabited by blacks and mestizos, not far from the slaughterhouse, with small houses which got poorer and smaller as they approached the pampa.[2] The family's social standing would be relatively poor rather than wealthy.

In 1816 the death of his father took place.[3] For Gutiérrez this was a factor in his deviations in youth from model behavior, since the widowed mother would be indulgent to a favorite son [4] (V, iv). Some scholars have seen an allusion to a harsh guardian who would appear to have taken on the role of father in a letter Esteban wrote to his brother José María, on March 22, 1826, in which he says that his spirit has dissipated in part the shadows infused in his childhood by a despot.[5] This seems to be somewhat slender evidence on which to base a theory; despotism might have been exerted on him by his father as well as by a guardian or tutor.

In any case, Echeverría seems not to have been proud of his youthful behavior. In a letter dated July 5, 1836 he says that when he was fifteen years old, love affairs, a divorce, and dagger-thrusts scandalized half the town, and that when he was eighteen, he was known by many as a gambler at billiards and a libertine (V, 452). In another passage, dated September 2, 1835, he states that up to the age of eighteen his life was almost wholly external, absorbed by sensations, love affairs, idle pursuits, passions of the blood, and upon occasion, meditation, but as sad as a lantern among tombs (V, 442). This seems to be the general background for his feeling that he was responsible for the death of his mother, which took place in 1822. This feeling he expresses in "Cartas a un amigo" ("Letters to a Friend") (V, 21–26). Although these passages may not be true autobiography, they convey vividly his affection for his mother and his probable remorse at having caused her death: "Una idea me atormenta: creo haber sido la causa involuntaria de la melancolía que la consume. Los halagos seductores de una mujer me arrastraron a algunos excesos; la ignorancia y la indiscreción propagaron y exageraron estos extravíos de mi inexperiencia: ella los supo y desde entonces data su enfermedad: calla por no afligirme, sin duda, pero yo he creído leer en su semblante mi acusación y mi martirio" (V, 23).

("One idea torments me: I think I have been the involuntary cause of the melancholy which consumes her. The seductive attractions of a woman brought me to certain excesses; ignorance and indiscretion spread and exaggerated these waywardnesses from my inexperience: she discovered them and since then dates her illness: she keeps silent so as not to grieve me, doubtless, but I think I have read in her countenance my accusation and my martyrdom.")

"Arrojéme sobre su cuerpo . . . imprimí mil y mil besos sobre su frío rostro y pareció animarse . . . ; recogió todas sus fuerzas y articuló estas palabras: 'Hijo, yo me muero: . . . Ya mi hora va a sonar: . . . No te

11

olvides de mis lecciones . . . Eres joven; no te dejes arrastrar por tus pasiones . . . El hombre debe abrigar aspiraciones elevadas. La Patria espera de sus hijos: ella es la única madre que te queda: A . . .' y la palabra expiró en su garganta . . ." (V, 24).

("I hurled myself on her . . . body, . . . I impressed thousands of kisses on her cold face and she seemed to revive; she gathered together all her strength and articulated these words: 'Son, I am dying: . . . Soon my hour is going to sound: . . . Don't forget the lessons I taught you . . . You are young; don't let yourself be led astray by your passions . . . Man should hold high aspirations. The homeland has expectations of its children: it is the only mother you have left: Ah . . . ' and the word expired in her throat . . .")

"Levantéme de cama; busqué a mi madre y no la encontré; estaba en el sepulcro. La eternidad la separaba de mí." (V, 25).

("I got up from bed; I looked for my mother and could not find her; she was in the tomb. Eternity separated her from me.")

"Ella expiró; pero su imagen está grabada aquí en mi corazón y en todas mis potencias con caracteres indelebles. Ella me consuela en mis sueños y me acompaña en todas partes. El hábito de verla y hablarla me lleva muchas veces a su cuarto: allí está la silla, el sofá, la mesa, la cama; pero todo desierto y silencioso . . ." (V, 26).

("She has expired; but her image is engraved here in my heart and in all my faculties with indelible letters. She consoles me in my dreams and accompanies me everywhere. The habit of seeing her and speaking to her takes me often to her room: there is the chair, the sofa, the table, the bed; but everything deserted and silent . . .")

Despite the strong emotionalism of these passages, it cannot be denied that the simplicity of expression (simpler in Spanish then in English translation, in which the need to choose a Latinate or a Germanic equivalent creates problems in tone, one word being too heavy and the other perhaps too common or undignified) creates a strong impression of real sincerity on Echeverría's part.

If the harsh guardian may account for Echeverría's hatred of tyranny, the beloved mother may be the cause of the idealization of woman, which is another of the hallmarks of his writing.

In his early years Echeverría became a capable musician; Gutiérrez suggests that he may have played his guitar to accompany the *cielito* or "little heaven," as the dance of the pampas is called, as performed in the suburbs of the southern part of Buenos Aires, before graduating to performing on the fine *vihuela*, dignified cousin of the guitar, made in Spain. Gutiérrez says that Echeverría was proud of belonging to the school of the Catalán Maestro Sor and of interpreting the learned music of Aguado, written especially for the *vihuela* [7] (V, xxix–xxx). Echeverría's musical skill was a key to his establishing rapport with the *gaucho*, with whom he might seem to have had little in common. Verse and music are intimately linked for the *gaucho*, and it is in the context of the love of music that the following reference to Echeverría was made by Sarmiento:

"El joven Echeverría residió algunos meses en la campaña, en 1840, y la fama de sus versos sobre la pampa le había precedido ya: los gauchos lo rodeaban con respeto y afición, y cuando un recién venido mostraba señales de desdén hacia el *cajetilla*, alguno le insinuaba al oído: 'Es poeta', y toda prevención hostil cesaba al oír este título privilegiado."[8]

("The young Echeverría lived for some months in the countryside, in 1840, and the fame of his verses on the pampa had gone before him: the *gauchos* gathered round him with respect and enjoyment, and when a recent arrival would show signs of scorn toward the elegant city-dweller, someone would let slip into his ear: 'He's a poet,' and every hostile prejudice would cease upon hearing this privileged title.")

His early education was at the school of the *cabildo* or town council in the *barrio* where he was born.[9]

II. Work and Study in Argentina, France, and England

In 1822 both Esteban Echeverría and his brother Félix were students in the department of preparatory studies of the new University of Buenos Aires, founded by Bernardino Rivadavia when he was prime minister, a few years before his brief and unfortunate term as president of the country.[10] During his two years there he studied Latin and philosophy. He obtained a certificate tesifying to his "repeated proofs of talent, judgment, and application."[11] Later on Echeverría criticized his philosophy teacher for spreading materialism and atheism among the youth.[12] Echeverría and his brother were also students of drawing under José Guth; the school of drawing was part of the Department of Exact Sciences of the same University.[13] Toward the end of 1823 Echeverría left his university studies to take a job as customs clerk in the establishment of Sebastián Lezica and Brothers, where he remained until September 20, 1825 (V, v–vi).

In his spare time he studied French and reached the point of being able to read with understanding history and poetry written in that language. According to Gutiérrez, Echeverría soon mastered French to perfection (V,vi).

Apparently the death of his mother, his study at the university, and the maturing process which his employment in business must have aided combined to suggest to him that he should go abroad to study. Sebastián Lezica and Félix Piñeyro are said to have encouraged him and to have helped him overcome the obstacles that were in the way of this European trip.

In October of 1825 he left Buenos Aires aboard a ship named the Joven Matilde or Young Matilda, if not Jenny.[14] He made stops at Bahia and Pernambuco in Brazil, and reached Le Havre in France on February 27, 1825, aboard the frigate Aquiles or Achilles (V,x). From Le Havre he went to Paris, arriving on March 6 (V, 449). The story of the months spent in Paris and England has not been amply documented, but the experience was an important part of the preparation for a literary and political career.

Echeverría's own statement, often quoted, certainly shows what he himself considered most important: "Durante mi residencia en Paris, y como desahogo a estudios más serios me dediqué a leer algunos libros de literatura. Shakespeare, Schiller, Goethe, y especialmente Byron me conmovieron profundamente y me revelaron un mundo nuevo. Entonces me sentí inclinado a poetizar; pero no conocía ni el idioma, ni el mecanismo de la metrificación española. Me dormía con el libro en la mano; pero haciendo esfuerzos sobre mí mismo, al cabo manejaba medianamente el verso" (V, 449). ("During my stay in Paris, and as relief from more serious studies I engaged in the reading of some books of literature. Shakespeare, Schiller, Goethe, and especially Byron moved me deeply and revealed a new world to me.[15] Then I felt an inclination in me to write poetry; but I knew neither the language nor the mechanics of Spanish versification. I used to fall asleep with my book in my hand; but exerting efforts on myself, finally I could halfway control verse.")

Echeverría studied mathematics, geography, drawing, and did reading and note-taking of such writers' works in philosophy, political science, and history as Pascal, Montesquieu, Leroux, Cousin, and Guizot (V, xvi).[16]

He also spent a month and a half in England, actually in London, according to his own statement (V, 449). According to Gutiérrez he had a profound knowledge of both English and French, particularly the latter (V, 413). This command of the two languages must have been reinforced and extended by his travel and it seems clear that his acquaintance with the work of French Romantics was stimulated by his French years.

III. Return to a Different Argentina

Early in May, 1830 Echeverría boarded the frigate Correo de las Indias at Le Havre; the ship stopped at Montevideo in June, and reached Buenos Aires in July (V, xxxii). [17]

Upon his return to his homeland, he devoted at least part of his energies to establishing a reputation as a poet. Perhaps he realized the effectiveness of looking like a poet in creating a reputation; Gutiérrez's description of him at this period suggests something of the sort. He says that Echeverría attracted interest wherever he went; he was a model of good and simple manners, he wore with the greatest possible naturalness clothing which showed itself by its tailoring to be a product of the skill of French craftsmen in sartorial art. He wore a gold-rimmed lens which he needed for distant objects, and nobody criticized him as affected when frequently in the street he would raise his hand to his eye to recognize people who attracted his attention (V, xxxiii–xxxiv).

An important factor in making his return to Argentina somewhat depressing was his poor health. Even before leaving for Europe, he had suffered from time to time palpitations or symptoms of discomfort in the region of the heart. Within a few months of his return to Buenos Aires, the malady—which had been quiescent during his sea voyages and residence abroad—became more severe, so much so that Echeverría felt his condition to be hopeless (V, xxxviii). With a friend, in November 1832, he sought improvement in his health by seeking out the beneficent waters, agreeable climate, and pure air up the river Uruguay to the city of Mercedes on the edge of the Río Negro. Six months there brought no real relief (V, xlv–xlvi). Poor health, the monocle and Paris-tailored attire, both accident and design combined to help the creation of a legend—Echeverría suggested the Byronic and poetic hero, beset by an adverse fate. In this period, that of literary Romanticism, Echeverría met the expectations of what a poet should be like. Echeverría admired Byron greatly, and had by intention and by circumstances the qualities of a hero in that pattern. A perceptive critic of Echeverría's poetry has stated the case as follows: ". . . entre los argentinos, la pasión byroniana se apoderó del hombre que por fatalidades de carácter interno y de carácter externo, pudo encarnar con propiedad perfecta el personaje byroniano: Esteban Echeverría."[18] (". . . among Argentinians, the Byronic passion took possession of the man who through circumstances of fate of internal and of external character, was able to embody with perfect propriety the Byronic character: Esteban Echeverría.")

When Echeverría left Argentina in 1825, the star of the progressive Unitarian Bernardino Rivadavia was high; when he returned in 1830, the despotic Federalist Juan Manuel de Rosas was in power. Echeverría, too, had changed, but as a result of having lived and studied in Paris, and having become enthusiastic about his Byronic qualities of poet, lover, political liberal, he was less prepared than ever to find an atmosphere of despotism congenial.

It is not surprising, then, to find him expressing sorrow at the changed political atmosphere of Buenos Aires. In an autobiographical fragment he speaks of the genesis of his first book of poems: "Después el retroceso degradante en que hallé a mi país, mis esperanzas burladas, produjeron en mí una melancolía profunda. Me encerré en mí mismo y de ahí nacieron infinitas producciones de las cuales no publiqué sino una mínima parte con el título de 'Consuelos' en el año 1834" (V, 449–450).

("Afterwards the degrading step backward in which I found my country, my hopes disappointed, produced in me a deep melancholy. I withdrew into myself and from that were born countless works of which I published only a minimal portion under the title of 'Consolations' in the year 1834.")

Even before publication of *Los consuelos (The Consolations)* some of his individual poems were published in Buenos Aires newspapers. In 1832 he published anonymously his narrative poem, *Elvira*, but the time was not propitious for literary works (V, xxxiv–xxxvi, xli–xlii). Some of the poems published separately earlier were included in *The Consolations*, which enjoyed success when published in 1834, under his own name (V, xlviii–xlix).

During these years, between 1832 and 1835, there was a brief respite from the direct rule of Rosas, but the situation was tense and Rosas's wife, Doña

15

Encarnación Ezcurra, was active in Buenos Aires while her husband was engaged in the expedition against the Indians. The lull before the storm may explain Echeverría's activity in the social life of Buenos Aires, at such salons as those of the popular Mariquita Sánchez, whose full name was María de Todos los Santos Sánchez de Velazco y Trillo. Her first husband was Martín Jacobo Thompson by whom she had a son, Juan Thompson, a close friend of Echeverría, and her second husband was Washington Mendeville, Consul of France. It is likely that at one of her salons the poet met the painter Carlos E. Pellegrini, to whom admirers of Echeverría are indebted for what has been described as the best of the portraits that exist of the poet.[19]

Music was an interest of Echeverría during much of his life. One of his activities was collaborative song writing, Echeverría providing texts for the music of a colleague. The most famous of his musical associates was Juan Pedro Esnaola.Their activity has been described as follows: "A juicio nuestro, los Sres. Echeverría y Esnaola, cuyas composiciones todos conocemos, pertenecen a ese venturoso número de seres que illustran a su patria . . . aquí el músico está a la par del poeta; ambos deben gloriarse de esta intimidad, de esa profunda relación intelectual que los liga . . ."[20] ("In our judgment, Messrs. Echeverría and Esnaola, whose compositions we all know, belong to that fortunate number of beings who do honor to their homeland . . . Here the musician is at a par with the poet; both must take pride in this intimacy, of that profound intellectual relationship that links them together . . .") In 1837–1838 José Antonio Wilde published four folders of songs under the title *Cancionero argentino (Argentinian Song Book)*; in this collection were included several songs with text by Echeverría.[21]

From 1835 on the University of Buenos Aires was adversely affected by attacks against it by the regime of Rosas; a series of repressive measures were passed that caused forced retirements and resignation of some of the professors. This had repercussions on the students who also were directly affected by such decrees as one obliging them to prove adherence to the national cause of the Federation, that is, to Rosas's party and purpose, prior to obtaining the doctorate. Limits thereby were placed on free inquiry and discussion within the University. Discussion was less restricted in organizations outside.

In 1832 the Association of Historical and Social Studies was founded; in June of 1837 a similar group was organized by a bookseller, Marcos Sastre, which held its meetings in a locale near his bookstore in the center of Buenos Aires. In a speech at the inauguration of this group, called the Literary Salon, Sastre set forth the purposes: to form a library, to give lessons and readings that would communicate the new ideas in religion, philosophy, agriculture, history, poetry, music, and painting. It held meetings once or twice a week on literature, philosophy, and art; its library contained recent books and newspapers or journals from Europe. Echeverría's new poem was introduced to the group by José María Gutiérrez, who read two cantos of "La cautiva" ("The Captive Woman") at meetings on June 26 and July 1 of 1837.[22]

An active role for Echeverría was suggested to him in a letter on the purposes of the Salon by Marcos Sastre: "Yo pienso, señor Echeverría, y me atrevo a asegurar, que Ud. está llamado a presidir y dirigir el desarrollo de la inteligencia de este país. Ud. es quien debe encabezar la marcha de la juventud; Ud. debe levantar el estandarte de los principios que deben guiarla, y que tanto necesita en el completo descarrío intelectual y literario en que hoy se encuentra. ¿No siente Ud., allá en su interior, un presentimiento de que está destinado a tanta y gloriosa misión?"[23] ("I think, Mr. Echeverría, and I presume to affirm, that you are called to preside and to direct the development of the intelligence of this country. You are the one who should head the progress of the youth; you should raise the banner of the principles that ought to guide it, and that it needs so much in the complete intellectual and literary waywardness in which it exists today. Do you not feel deep down inside you a presentiment that you are destined to so great and glorious a mission?")

Here began the active role of Echeverría in guiding the youth of his country; the legend would help him. Unfortunately the Literary Salon, with its progressive goals, could not flourish openly, and secrecy became necessary. In January, for a variety of reasons but chiefly the political situation, it was decided to close the Literary Salon.[24]

Echeverría, however, and others were able to reorganize in a secret organization, an Association of the Young Argentinian Generation, similar to European Romantic youth organizations of the era. On June 23, 1838 its first meeting was held, and on July 9, 1838 they swore to the principles of their Credo, largely composed by Echeverría.

Meanwhile Echeverría had published his *Rimas (Rhymes)* that contained "The Captive Woman" as its longest poem; this took place in 1837 (V, li).

Gutiérrez has described Echeverría's goals and those of the Association as basic and peaceful, leading to a future regeneration of the homeland by means of all good citizens, all interest, all opinions (V, lxii–lxiii). Rosas's police learned the secret of the meetings of the Association; to continue them would have been to court disaster (V, lxv). Some members left the country, but Echeverría opted to withdraw to the ranch or *estancia* of Los Talas, which had been established by his brother (V, lxvi–lxvii).

While he was there, two events occurred, as mentioned in the first chapter on the geography and history of Echeverría's homeland: the liberal revolt at Chascomús, which became the subject of one of his narrative poems, and the invasion of General Juan Lavalle, opposing Rosas, from the North (V, lxvi, lxix. General Lavalle's troops occupied the area where Los Talas was located and Echeverría had to choose between support of the ill-starred general, whom he designated as "a sword without head" in his poem *Avellaneda*, and passing over to the ranks of the hated despot, Rosas. He cast his lot with General Lavalle, and elaborated with a friend an anti-Rosas document reproduced by Gutiérrez, in which was stated among other things that Rosas was an abominable tyrant who had usurped the rule of the people and that nobody was obliged to obey his orders. Lavalle was killed in defeat in mid-September of 1841 (V, lxx–lxxii). Echeverría's poor health and physical weakness prevented him from joining Lavalle's army to fight or to retreat; he was forced by Lavalle's defeat to flee with the clothes he was wearing, leaving behind even his manuscripts as well as a future in his homeland, to emigrate to Uruguay as a refugee (V, lxxiii).

IV. Exile in Uruguay; the Struggle Continues; Death Intervenes

On a French ship Echeverría was able to leave Argentina to take refuge for some months at Colonia del Sacramento. In June of 1841 he went to Montevideo where he shared the difficulties confronting the defenders of the city against the siege (V, lxxiii, lxxvi).[25] Among the defenders was the man who would later play a decisive part in achieving the independence of Italy, Giuseppe Garibaldi. Echeverría did not take an active part in defending Montevideo, since he felt that the only way to overthrow Rosas was by revolution within Argentina headed by the *caudillos*. His valor was beyond question, as Gutiérrez tells us, using as proof the story of an alarm motivated by a threat from the besiegers which brought Echeverría to the fighting with his weapons; later, when he was going back home, wrapped in his cape and bent by the weight of his physical ills, he was overtaken by General Pacheco y Obes, leading his cavalry. The general took off his hat to Echeverría and paid tribute to the poet for giving so fine an example of abnegation and constancy (V, lxxviii–lxxix). Echeverría, unlike some of his fellow Unitarian exiles, sought more than an overthrow of Rosas (or a restoration of liberal Unitarian rule); he sought a regeneration on the basis of a set of beliefs, or a doctrine, such as was exemplified in his Credo, published in revised form in Montevideo as the *Dogma socialista (Socialist Dogma)* in 1846 (V, lxxx).[26]

Much of his energy went into his completion of narrative poems: the *Insurrección del Sur (Insurrection of the South)*, *La guitarra (The Guitar)*, *Avellaneda*, and *El ángel caído (The Fallen Angel)*, or, in some cases, their publication.

In 1846 he published the *Manual de enseñanza moral para las escuelas primarias (Manual of Moral Instruction for the Primary Schools* (V, lxxxvi, lxxxviii–xci).[27]

He also published in 1848 a study on the revolution in February of that year in France.[28]

The story of the polemic with José Rivera Indarte, editor of *El Nacional*, throws light on Echeverría's sensitivity. In April of 1844, Echeverría was invited by Andrés Lamas, political chief of Montevideo, to take part in the poetry ceremony to be held on the May 25 anniversary in the Theater of Commerce. Argentina's independence and Montevideo's heroic struggle (as a New Troy) were to be celebrated by the best poets of the city. Lamas, who was also president of the National Historical Institute, began by speaking of the significance of May (i.e., Argentina's independence) and announcing that soon would appear Esteban Echeverría's work on primary education. Echeverría had prepared a speech on May and popular instruction in the River Plate region but, because of some confusion, was not asked to deliver it. Six poets read their poems for the occasion and the applause was particularly heated for those of Luis Domínguez, author of a very famous poem on the *ombú*, lonely and huge tree of the pampa, and of Echeverría, for whom it would appear to have been a solid triumph. In *El Nacional*, the editor "out of modesty" refused to mention his own poetic contribution, and spoke of the deep impression made on him by the poems of Francisco Acuña de Figueroa and by Bartolomé Mitre, with no reference to Echeverría's poem.

Someone, perhaps a friend of the poet, using the pen name, *Un Oriental*, an Oriental (in this era, Oriental corresponds to Uruguayan, resident of the East Bank), wrote to express surprise at the omission of all reference to Echeverría's poem which had won such favor from the public. Rivera Indarte then went to visit Echeverría to present his excuses, did not find him at home, and left them in writing. In *El Nacional* of May 31, he published the letter of an Oriental, and an explanation, in which he said that the evening was patriotic rather than literary, that the applause was for the sacred words of the dogma, without regard to critical approval or censure. He went on to say that among those present were some who had given proof of their attitudes [*sic*] as writers of prose and verse and who did not recognize in what surrounded them a lance so well tempered that it might be able to break the armor of their merits. If this seems to be ambiguous, it was undoubtedly so intended. Rivera Indarte also referred directly to Echeverría saying that he had introduced to them the new poetry, initiated by writers like Mme de Staël and Chateaubriand, continued by Byron, Victor Hugo, and others, that is, Romanticism, and that with his composition in honor of May on that occasion had worthily begun his campaign against Rosas. This was calculated to infuriate Echeverría, particularly the implication that up to 1844, Echeverría had not begun his attacks on Rosas.

In *El Constitutional* of June 1 appeared Echeverría's reply. Rivera Indarte invited Echeverría to give proofs that he had, indeed, begun the attacks on Rosas before Rivera Indarte; Echeverría replied with even greater anger. To this came one more letter from each side. One year later Rivera Indarte died at the age of thirty-nine in Brazil.[29] It is gratifying to record that Echeverría praised him in his account of the genesis of the Credo published in 1846: "El malogrado D. José Rivera Indarte hizo con constancia indomable cinco años la guerra al tirano de su patria. —Sólo la muerte pudo arrancar de su mano la enérgica pluma con que el Nacional acusaba ante el Mundo al exterminador de los Argentinos. La Europa lo oyó aunque tarde, cuando caía exánime bajo el peso de las fatigas, como al pie de sus banderas el valiente soldado" (IV, 68). ("The unfortunate Don José Rivera Indarte carried on with indomitable constancy for five years his war against the tyrant of his homeland. —Only death could snatch from his hand the energetic pen with which *El Nacional* accused before the world the exterminator of the Argentinians. Europe heard him, though too late, when he was falling unconscious beneath the weight of his fatigues, like the valiant soldier beneath his banners.")

The meeting between Domingo Faustino Sarmiento and Echeverría in Montevideo has interest both because of the fame of the two compatriots, and also because of the light it sheds on the subject of this study:

"To make up for so many losses, I met Echeverría, a gentle man and an ardent poet. My friendship with him saved me many hours of boredom in the besieged city. What animated talks we had about what was happening on the other side of the river! . . . . Contemplation of nature and the influence of beauty have elevated his soul . . . he suffers morally and physically and awaits the outcome without hope of being able to return to his country and devote himself to his beautiful theories of liberty and justice."[30] Sarmiento reached Montevideo in late 1845.

Echeverría's death took place on January 19, 1851 at ten o'clock in the morning in his bare room on the street named Misiones in Montevideo. He had for a long time expected death; he was in full mental power. The government had to pay his funeral expenses since he left nothing but manuscripts. Rosas is supposed to have said when he learned of Echeverría's death: "One enemy less."[31]

He was buried in the Cemetery of the Parent House in Montevideo. His remains disappeared and could not be found when the attempt was made to remove them to Buenos Aires for reburial.[32]

CHAPTER 3

THE NARRATIVE POEMS

"In the year 1834, Esteban Echeverría, one of Argentina's foremost men of letters, published a literary credo, applied by him to Spanish American poetry but by his successors to every branch of their literature. This proclamation is one of the milestones of Spanish American literary criticism and cannot therefore be omitted, however often it has been quoted."[1] As Theodore Andersson states, Echeverría made the proclamation in question with regard to poetry; it is the need for the New World Spanish poets to provide their work with a process of localizing, of Argentinizing, of Americanizing, if the words may be so used, their compositions. It will be a convenience to let Echeverría's words, flowery though they may seem, repeat their message here:

> La poesía entre nosotros aun no ha llegado a adquirir el influjo y prepotencia moral que tuvo en la antigüedad, y que hoy goza entre las cultas naciones europeas: preciso es, si quiere conquistarla, que aparezca revestida de un carácter propio y original, y que reflejando los colores de la naturaleza física que nos rodea, sea a la vez el cuadro vivo de nuestras costumbres, y la expresión más elevada de nuestras ideas dominantes, de los sentimientos y pasiones que nacen del choque inmediato de nuestros sociales intereses, y en cuya esfera se mueve nuestra cultura intelectual. Sólo así, campeando libre de los lazos de toda extraña influencia, nuestra poesía llegará a ostentarse sublime como los Andes; peregrina, hermosa y varia en sus ornamentos como la fecunda tierra que la produzca (III,12).
>
> (Poetry among us still has not reached the point of acquiring the influence and moral power that it had in ancient times, and which it enjoys today among the cultivated European nations: it is necessary, if it wishes to gain it, that it appear clad in an original character appropriate to it, and that reflecting the colors of the physical nature that surrounds us, it become at the same time the living portrait of our customs, and the most elevated expression of our ruling ideas, of the sentiments and passions that are born from the immediate collision of our social interests, and in the sphere of which moves our intellectual culture. Only thus, making its way free of the bonds of every foreign influence, our poetry will succeed in displaying itself as sublime as the Andes; rare, beautiful, and varied in its ornaments like the fertile earth producing it.)

It is noteworthy that this Americanization should be present physically (reflecting the physical nature of the environment), socially (reflecting customs in a lifelike manner), and intellectually (reflecting the expression of the ideas). Not all aspects of Echeverría's literary credo have been followed by later Spanish American writers, but one or more of his suggestions has been present in the work of many of his successors, whether or not they have consciously found their purpose in his example. It will be convenient, in any case, to keep these points in mind in assessing the merits of Echeverría's work, particularly when considering his poetry.

The long poem, rather than the lyric, Echeverría felt, was calculated to effect the mission designed by him. This he expressed as follows: "En poesía, para mí, las composiciones cortas siempre han sido de muy poca importancia caulquiera que sea su mérito. Para que la poesía pueda llenar dignamente su misión profética; para que pueda obrar sobre las masas y ser un poderoso elemento social, y no como hasta aquí entre nosotros y nuestros padres, un pasatiempo fútil, y, cuando más, agradable, es necesario que la poesía sea bella, grande, sublime y se manifieste bajo formas colosales" (V,xlv). ("In poetry, for me, short compositions always have been of very slight importance, whatever their merit may be. For poetry to be able to fulfill worthily its prophetic mission, for it to be able to work on the masses and be a powerful social element, and not as up to the present among us and our fathers, a futile pastime, and, at the most, agreeable, it is necessary for poetry to be beautiful, great, sublime and manifest itself under colossal forms.")

Short poetic compositions, then, may have merit, but to achieve something of importance, the longer narrative poem, in the tradition of a Byron, or a Goethe, appears to be the vehicle favored by Echeverría. It is appropriate, then, in assessing the achievement of him as a poet to consider first his narrative poems, to which the term *leyenda* or "legend" might sometimes appropriately be given, a term applied to the longer narrative poems of the Romantic writers who wrote in Spanish—writers like the Duque de Rivas in Spain.

I. A Tentative, Anonymous Beginning

A dedicatory note to Dr. José María Fonseca, which was not included in the anonymously published *Elvira*, dated June 28, 1832 gives Echeverría's statement about the poem. Some passages are worthy of notice: ". . . le envío a *ELVIRA* con todos sus defectos y deformidades, . . . No debe usted extrañar la debilidad de esta obra, por que ha sido concebida en una época aciaga para mí . . . Excuso hablarle de las novedades introducidas en mi poema, y de que no hallará modelo ninguno en la poesía castellana, siendo su origen la poesía del siglo, la poesía romántica Inglesa, Francesa y Alemana, por que usted está tan al corriente como yo (V, 150–151). ("I send you *ELVIRA* with all its defects and deformities . . . You must not be surprised at the feebleness of this work, because it has been conceived in an ill-omened epoch for me . . . I don't have to mention to you the novelties introduced into my poem, and for which you will find no model in Castilian poetry, since their origin is the poetry of the century, the English, French, and German romantic poetry, because you are as up to date as I."

If Echeverría's purpose in the Americanization of a narrative poem physically, socially, and intellectually be kept in mind, it is clear that Echeverría cannot be awarded high marks for this apprenticelike work. The chief American characteristic is the location of the poem's action, made clear by the subtitle which identifies Elvira as *la novia del Plata*, "the sweetheart of the (River) Plate."

The poem, dedicated to Dr. Fonseca, is divided into twelve sections, differing in rhymes (both assonance and consonance are found), their schemes, numbers of stanzas, number of verses in stanzas, and numbers of syllables per line. The metrical variety is one of the characteristic features of the Romantic *leyenda* or narrative poem, partly because of the probability that interest may be heightened by variation, and partly because of the feeling that effects of versification can reinforce the poem's emotional content. Echeverría was conscious of this; he has stated:

> El ritmo es la música por medio de la cual la poesía cautiva los sentidos y habla con más eficiacia al alma. Ya vago y pausado él remeda el reposo y las cavilaciones de la melancolía; ya sonoro, precipitado y veloz, la tormenta de los afectos.
>
> El diestro tañedor con él modula en todos los tonos del sentimiento y se eleva al sublime concierto del entusiasmo y de la pasión: con una disonancia hiere, con una armonía hechiza, y por medio de la consonancia silábica y onomatopéyica de los sonidos da voz a la naturaleza inanimada, y hace fluctuar el alma entre el recuerdo y la esperanza pareando y alternando sus *Rimas*" (V, 119). ("Rhythm is the music by means of which poetry captivates the senses and speaks with most efficacy to the soul. When indeterminate and deliberate it imitates repose and the ruminations of melancholy; when sonorous, precipate and swift, the torment of the affections.
>
> The skilled player with it modulates in all the tones of feeling and elevates himself to the sublime harmony with enthusiasm and passion: with a dissonance he wounds, with a harmony he bewitches, and by means of syllabic and onomatopeic harmony of the sounds gives voice to inanimate nature, and causes the soul to fluctuate between reminiscence and hope matching and alternating his *Rhymes*.")

As example of appropriate skill in the employment of techniques of versification, Echeverría refers to Coleridge in his "Ancient Mariner."[2] He states of Coleridge's language that it is "impetuoso y rápido como la tempestad que impele al bajel, y cuando la calma se acerca se muestra solemne y majestuoso" (V, 120). (". . . impetuous and rapid as the storm which forces the vessel ahead, and when the calm approaches it becomes solemn and majestic.")

Echeverría experiments with some success in this regard. For example, there is a storm which accompanies the appearance of the spirits of Hell upon the scene, in order to participate in a Walpurgis Night. The choppy succession of octosyllables creates the effect of rapidity and impetuosity that is completely appropriate:

> Del espeso bosque prado,
> De la tierra, el aire, el cielo,
> Al fulgor de fátuas lumbres
> Con gran murmullo salieron

Sierpes, Grifos y Demonios,
Partos del hórrido averno,
Vampiros, Gnomos y Larvas,
Trasgos, lívidos espectros,
Animas en pena errantes,
Vanas sombras y Esqueletos . . . (I, 20)
(From the dense forest and meadow,
From the earth, the air, the sky,
To the gleam of wills of the wisp
With great rustling came out
Snakes, griffins and demons,
Creations of horrid Avernus,
Vampires, gnomes and larvae,
Goblins, livid spectres,
Wandering souls in torment,
Vain shades and skeletons . . .)

Even in literal translation the rapid succession of the creatures' names retains some of the vigor of the original. After the scene of excitement is ended, the mood changes, and instead of octosyllables the poet has recourse to hendecasyllables and heptasyllables, which permit the suggestion of relative calm, and majesty: "En su trono de fuego el Mediodía / Reinaba rutilante y majestuoso, / Y Lisardo infeliz desde la aurora; / Sumergido yacía / En letargo profundo y silencioso" (I, 21). ("On his throne of fire Midday / Reigned shining and majestic, / And Lisardo unhappy since dawn / Lay submerged / In deep and silent lethargy.") In the first passage there are eighty syllables; in the second fifty-one. There are twenty-four sibilants in the first passage as opposed to eleven in the second passage. In each of the octosyllables there are three stressed syllables, just as there are in each of the hendecasyllables; thus, the proportion of stressed syllables to unstressed ones in the first passage is relatively high. The proportion is demonstrably lower in the second passage. This may not be unusual, but certainly shows that Echeverría was conscious of possibilities in the use of devices of versification, and that even in this early poem he displayed a certain mastery in appropriate variation.

The introduction of a Walpurgis Night scene corresponds better to the desire of Echeverría to turn away from Castilian tradition and embrace the European Romantic innovations of writers like Hugo. Gutiérrez felt that this was a mistake, that Echeverría was victim to the fashion of his day: "Echeverría pagó tributo a su época. El genio de las tinieblas, Lucifer, ataviado con cetro y tiara, presidiendo fiestas sabáticas, los espíritus foletos, las almas errantes constituyen parte del mundo invisible, la región de los pavores místicos, en el sistema del autor de *Elvira*, a usanza de los poetas artistas de la escuela de Goethe y de V. Hugo" (V, lxvi). ("Echeverría paid tribute to his epoch. The genius of the darkness, Lucifer, dressed up with sceptre and tiara, presiding over Walpurgis night festivals, the hobgoblins, the wandering souls constitute part of the invisible world, the region of mystical

terrors, in the system of the author of *Elvira*, in the manner of poet artists
of the school of Goethe and V. Hugo.")

A frequent characteristic of Romantic verse is the use of epigraphs; they
link a work to that of other poets, they serve to emphasize the theme or
thought of a poem, they display the familiarity of the poet with works from
which the epigraph is chosen, they invest their authority on the new work—
these are some of the possible functions of an epigraph. In this case, there
are two epigraphs. The first is from a *silva* (a Spanish stanza type) written
by Nicolás Fernández de Moratín (1737–1780) on occasion of a royal wed-
ding: "Ven, Himeneo, ven. Ven Himeneo." (come, Hymen, come. Come,
Hymen.)[3] (I, 3) The second epigraph is the first line of a poem by William
Wordsworth, "'Tis said that some have died for love."[4] These two epigraphs suggest the division of the poem into two parts: one part leading up
to the eighth section of the poem, wherein Elvira relates to her beloved
Lisardo a dream that she has had:

> El Himeneo
> Iba a enlazarlos
> Con el anillo
> Del puro amor,
> Y ellos ardientes
> Se encaminaban
> A la ara augusta
> Del sacro Dios:
> Mas de repente
> El negro brazo
> De un esqueleto
> Que apareció,
> Su mano en medio
> De los dos pechos
> Puso, y con furia
> Los separó" (I, 16–17).

("Hymen was going to unite them [two hearts] with the ring of pure love,
and they ardently were making their way to the august altar of the sacred
God: But suddenly the black arm of a skeleton appeared, put his hand between the two breasts and furiously separated them.") The dream is significant, and Elvira dies. Lisardo also dies, with a grief-stricken shriek: "Elvira, Elvira" (I, 31). Thus the epigraph of Wordsworth anticipates the
conclusion of the poem.

One of the more effective notes in the melancholy poem is the appearance
of a song, which makes up the sixth section of the poem, dealing with a
tender shrub carried off in winter by the swollen river near it; a desert rose,
destroyed by the wind; the death of hope and of love through the vicissitudes
of fortune. These octosyllables, in their simplicity, suggest a genuinely popular song text; the following section begins with hendecasyllables, and contrasts with Elvira's song, both metrically and textually.

Lisardo, it has been pointed out, bears a resemblance to the protagonist of Byron's poem, "Manfred,"[5] in his exploration of the field of science (I, 7).

Elvira possesses some historical significance as an early, possibly the first, full-fledged Romantic work published in Spanish America before the appearance of a similar work in Spain.[6] One critic has thought that Echeverría deserved the epithet of "Rubén Darío of American Romanticism," Darío being the man who more than any other established Modernism in the Hispanic poetic world in the late nineteenth century, for this work.[7] It brings into the literature of Latin America something of the feeling of the works of German, French, and English Romanticism; it deserves, on the other hand, some criticism for its lack of local color. Similarities between *Elvira* and the Spanish Romantic José de Espronceda's *El estudiante de Salamanca (The Student of Salamanca)* probably derive from influences shared by the two authors, rather than to the direct influence of one on the other.[8] Echeverría himself seems not to have been satisfied with the poem, but even so was hurt by its lack of critical success, and attacked his critics in a satirical poem.[9] It deserves sympathetic evaluation for its metrical variety and sincerity in describing an idealized star-crossed love.

II. The River Plate Serves As Tomb to an Unhappy Beauty

The legend *Layda* forms part of the volume of *Consolations* published by Echeverría in 1834. Thus, it is not anonymous, and may represent progress made by the poet in his attempt to place European Romanticism in the South American environment. The River Plate moves from its place in the subtitle of *Elvira* into the body of the poem, and there are other signs that the poet is making the narrative an Argentinian story. We meet the *pampero*, or "strong wind blowing over the pampas from the Andes" (III, 144). The sleeping currents of the River Plate are crossed by a ship which is making its way from the shores inhabited by the Argentinian (III, 149). Later on, as the climax comes, winds lash the currents of the river, bringing terror and violence with it, and death to the fair Layda; the poet beseeches the nymphs of the River Plate to weep tears of grief and of tenderness (III, 156). The eight parts of this poem occupy fourteen pages in the Gutiérrez edition, whereas the twelve sections of *Elvira* occupy twenty-eight pages. *Layda* is briefer, more economical, and possesses the same sort of poetic skill, variety of meters, and ability to evoke in metrically apposite verses different moods of Nature. The description of the storm over the river shows an ability to use onomatopeia:

> . . . levantaba
> El río soberano embravecido
> Su aterrador bramido,
> Y al sonoro rugido de los vientos,
> De los truenos y rayos lo mezclaba,

Con el ímpetu ciego de un torrente,
De su hidrópico seno vomitando
Sobre las ondas, ondas, que espumeando
El límite asaltaban prepotente,
Bramaban, se agitaban, resurtían
Y con nueva pujanza lo embestían — (III, 155).

("The mighty river made rough raised its terrifying roar, and to the sonorous howling of the winds, thunder, and lightning added it, with the blind rush of a torrent, spewing from its dropsical bosom other waves which as they foamed assaulted the powerful limit, roared, twisted, fell back and attacked it with new vigor.")

Once again, two epigraphs aid in the division of the poem into two main sections. First is one from Calderón: "Fue como ninguna bella,/ Y fue infeliz como todas"[10] (III, 143). "She was more beautiful than anyone, and was unhappy like all (women)." The other one is from "Dar-Thula" in Ossian's poems, in which Dar-Thula is looking for her beloved: "Where art thou, son of my love?; The roar of the blast is around me. / Dark is the cloudy night."[11] Echeverría also supplies a translation into Spanish of the English passage, as he had not for the Wordsworth epigraph for *Elvira* (III, 143).

Comparison between *Elvira* and *Layda* may serve to put into focus Echeverría's control of the narrative form. First, with regard to the title, both are names of a woman. Elvira is a frequent Spanish name, and is that of a number of Romantic heroines; Layda has been taken to suggest an Ossianic name.[12] The naming of the poem after Layda, a widow who, after the death of her child, is drowned when a storm causes her ship to sink in the waters of the River Plate, is appropriate, since she is the center of attention. Interestingly enough, the use of this rather un-Hispanic name as a title seems to have puzzled Gutiérrez, who altered it to "La ida," "the departure."[13] In the case of *Elvira*, two lovers, she and Lisardo share the scene almost equally; the choice of the woman's name as the main title may have been governed by the desire of Echeverría to link his poem to Romantic poems concerning brides. Echeverría's subtitle for *Elvira* is *la novia del Plata*, "the bride of the River Plate." The title is ambiguous; "bride" might be "fiancée" or "sweetheart," and *del Plata* might suggest that the heroine drowned in the river, as well as that she lived near it. The subtitle, if the content of the poem is kept in mind, corresponds closely to such famous works of Romanticism as Schiller's "Die Braut von Messina" ("The Bride of Messina"), 1803; Byron's "The Bride of Abydos," 1813; and Sir Walter Scott's "The Bride of Lammermoor," 1819, drama, poem, and novel respectively, and merely indicates the locale. Even in English the word "bride" may be used in the sense of "fiancée," as an editor of Byron's poem has reminded us. Byron found it hard to answer the question as to why his poem bore the title it did, since in the poem the heroine was only an intended bride. According to this editor, "The term is particularly applied on the day of marriage and during the 'honeymoon,' but is frequently used from the proclamation of the banns . . . In the debate on Prince Leopold's allowance, Mr. Gladstone, being criticized for speaking of the Princess Helena as the 'bride,' said he believed that colloquially a lady when engaged was often called a 'bride.'"[14] If Echeverría, as is likely, equated the word "bride" with *novia*, he would have found no problem in the fact that neither Elvira, his *novia*, nor Byron's "bride of Abydos," reached the altar. Schiller's play has something in common with Echeverría's poem in the device of an ominous dream which is fulfilled unhappily.[15]

Both poems are introduced by two epigraphs; both poems have one epigraph from the Spanish pre-romantic seventeenth or eighteenth century tradition (Calderón and the older Moratín) and one from the English Romantic or pre-Romantic tradition (Wordsworth and Ossian). In both the note of Romanticism is strong, but there are neoclassic elements, such as the reference to Hymen in *Elvira* and the reference to the nymphs of the river (the nymphs of the River Tagus in Portugal of which Camoëns was so fond come to mind) in *Layda* are examples. In both poems the Argentinian setting is established by the presence of the great river, but in *Layda* the localization or Americanization is clearer; the episode of *Layda* might have taken place— *Elvira* has more of the fantastic, and the location in Echeverría's homeland is not essential to the content of the poem. From the point of view of versification, both poems have lines of five, seven, eight, and eleven syllables, and in both poems the poet displays his desire and ability to make the music of the verse appropriate to the shifting moods of the text. Only in *Elvira* is assonance used; in that poem the ballad meter in assonance is associated strongly with the supernatural, which is not present in *Layda*. The use of ballad meter in *Elvira* may have been a conscious device of the poet to heighten the mood of mystery.[16]

With specific reference to Echeverría's next narrative poem, *The Captive Woman*, Sarmiento has suggested the marked change for the better from the preceding Neoclassicists; part of the change is in the infusion of Romantic elements, but perhaps more important for the South American of the first half of the nineteenth century is the emphasis on the local setting. To quote from Echeverría's great contemporary:

> Este bardo argentino dejó a un lado a Dido y Argía, que sus predecesores los Varela trataron con maestría clásica y estro poético, pero sin suceso y sin consecuencia, porque nada agregaban al caudal de nociones europeas, y volvió sus miradas al desierto, y allá en la inmensidad sin límites, en las soledades en que vaga el salvaje, en la lejana zona de fuego, que el viajero ve acercarse cuando los campos se incendian, halló las inspiraciones que proporciona a la imaginación, el espectáculo de una naturaleza solemne, grandiosa, inconmensurable, callada; y entonces, el eco de sus versos pudo hacerse oír con aprobación, aun por la península española.[17]

("This Argentinian bard put to one side Dido and Argia [titles and subjects of Neoclassical plays] treated with classical mastery and poetic inspiration by his predecessors the Varelas [two brothers named Florencio and Juan

Cruz], but without result and without consequence, because they added nothing to the abundance of European notions, and turned his gaze to the desert, and there in the limitless immensity, in the solitudes in which the savage wanders, in the distant zone of fire which the wayfarer sees approaching when the fields are set on fire, he found the inspirations which are given to the imagination by the spectacle of a solemn, grandiose, incommensurable, silent Nature; and then, the echo of his verses could make themselves heard with approval, even by the Spanish peninsula.") For Sarmiento, it is clear, it is the introduction of the physical environment of Argentina that is the most important factor in the success of Echeverría. And it may well be that this is the explanation for the relative lack of success of *Elvira* and of *Layda* when they are compared with *The Captive Woman*.

III. *Significance of the Title*

Ezequiel Martínez Estrada, one of "the four greatest Argentine writers of the first half of the twentieth century,"[18] has discussed the title of Echeverría's *The Captive Woman*: "*La cautiva* inicia en la literatura hispanoamericana los asuntos de ambiente, . . . bajo el vocabulario y el énfasis de la poesía española en boga. Además de esa originalidad posee otra: la de colocar en el primer plano heroico a una mujer. El título ya anuncia la novedad y un equivoco, pues el cautiverio no había ocupado nunca un primer lugar en esta clase de relatos; y, por otra parte, debió haberse titulado *El cautivo*, que es Brian, a quien liberta su amante . . ."[19] ("*The Captive Woman* initiates in Hispanoamerican literature affairs related to environment, with the vocabulary and emphasis of the fashionable Spanish poetry. Besides that originality it possesses another one: that of putting a woman in the chief heroic plane. The title already announces the novelty and an ambiguity, for captivity had never occupied a prominent place in this class of narratives; and, moreover, it ought to have been called *The Captive Man*, who is Brian, liberated by his beloved.") Here we see the names of the hero and heroine of the poem, but the English translation does not catch the connotation of the words *cautiverio*, "captivity," *cautiva*, "captive woman," and *cautivo*, "captive man." For Argentina, these words suggest a specific type of event associated with the long struggle with the Indian at the shifting frontier, a living issue in the day of Echeverría. The captive was a person who fell prisoner to the Indians or was carried off during the *malón*, "Indian raid." These were submitted to shameful servitude; a standard encyclopedia explains the term and provides an interesting example, dated 1870.[20] In translation, the example from Lucio Victorio Mansilla"s *Una excursión a los indios ranqueles* reads: "The captives are considered among the Indians as things. Imagine what their condition must be. All the same are the adult and the adolescent, the boy and the girl, white and black; they all are equal from the first moments until they make themselves liked as they inspire complete confidence. They must wash, cook, gather firewood in the forest with their hands, build corrals, tame the colts, care for the cattle and serve as instrument for the brutal pleasure of lust. Woe to those who try to resist!"[21]

Jorge Luis Borges has a page headed "El cautivo" ("The Captive Boy"); the age of the captive determines the choice of the word "man" or "boy" in translation, the gender of the noun, indicated by the vowel of the ending, the sex. As soon as the account of the incident begins, the reference becomes clear: "En Junín o en Tapalquén refieren la historia. Un chico desapareció después de un malón; se dijo que lo habían robado los indios."[22] ("In Junín or in Tapalquén they tell the story. A boy disappeared after a raid; it was said that the Indians had abducted him.") English readers confronted by the word "captive" lack associations with the word possessed by readers in Argentina of the nineteenth and twentieth centuries.[23]

IV. Epigraphs and Organization of the Poem

Not only does Echeverría make use of the epigraph, as in *Elvira* and *Layda*, at the beginning of his new poem, but in "The Captive Woman" the title and each section are provided with epigraphs that serve to emphasize and clarify their content and artistic purpose.[24]

That Echeverría felt that the epigraph had an important function may be inferred from a statement he made at the beginning of his "Proyecto o prospecto de una obra periódica" ("Project or Prospectus for a Periodical Work") to the effect that the epigraph indicates to the reader the target of the writer's quill (V, 175).

The title of the poem, already shown to require some explanation, is "The Captive Woman." There is no doubt that María, a woman, is the leading character of the poem, which might have caused Echeverría to have this poem follow the pattern of *Elvira* and *Layda*, by naming it "María." Rather than she, it is her husband, Brian, who suffers captivity or capture by the Indians; she rescues him, so that "The Captive Man," with regard to imprisonment is more appropriate than "The Captive Woman," with respect to the plot. The epigraph, part of Byron's *Don Juan*, reads as follows: "Female hearts are such a genial soil / For kinder feelings, whatsoe'er their nation, / They naturally pour the 'wine and oil' / Samaritans in every situation."[25] Echeverría provides a Spanish translation for his readers (1, 33). This passage does call attention to one aspect of María's character and amplifies the title. The reader is thereby prepared to find María the dominant figure in the poem.

There are nine parts and an epilogue, more or less equal in length and importance.

The epigraph to part one, "El desierto," (" The desert") (I, 35) is given only in French: "Ils vont. L'espace est grand." ("They go. The space is great.") Its author, Victor Hugo, is identified; Echeverría has begun his poem with epigraphs from two of the great Romantic poets: Byron of England, and Hugo of France. This part of the poem depicts the great expanse of the Argentine pampas. In Hugo's poem, the reference is to the rider Mazeppa and his horse; in the Spanish poem it is to a group of savage Indians on horseback. The words selected are appropriate to either context.[26]

The epigraph to part two, "El festín" ("The feast") (I, 45) is given only in Italian: ". . . orribile favelle, / Parole di dolore, accenti d'ira, / Voci alte e fioche, e suon di man con elle / Facevan un tumulto . . ." (". . . horrible utterances, words of woe, accents of anger, voices high and faint and sounds of hands with them, were making a tumult . . .")[27] Here is a passage from the world-famous narrative poem, the *Divine Comedy* of Dante; this, then, is the wild Hellish celebration of the savage Indians after their raid, in the course of which a number of captives have been taken.

The epigraph to part three, "El puñal" ("The dagger") (I, 57) is the first one from a Spanish source: "Yo iba a morir es verdad, / Entre bárbaros crueles, / Y allí el pesar me mataba / De morir, mi bien, sin verte. / A darme la vida tú / Saliste, hermosa, y valiente" (I, 57). ("I was going to die it is true, among cruel barbarians, and there suffering was killing me from dying, my treasure, without seeing you. You appeared, beautiful one, and courageous, to give me life.") This is taken from Calderón's play, *La Puente de Mantible (The Bridge of Mantible)*, a passage wherein Guido de Borgoña declares his debt to his beloved Floripes, sister to the Moor Fierabrás.[28] María, in this part of the poem, beautiful and courageous like Floripes, uses her dagger to cut her husband's bonds after she kills an Indian *cacique* or chief and helps him to escape with her. Brian, like Guido, recognizes the courage of his beloved: "Tu valor me infunde fuerza . . ." ("Your courage infuses strength in me") (I, 68).

A rather interesting reminiscence of the epigraph used for part one of the poem is made by Echeverría, when he speaks of María and Brian as they set out onto the pampas, and states in different stanzas: "Ellos van . . ." (I, 69) ("They go . . .") and "Ellos van.—Vasto, profundo / Como el páramo del mundo / Misterioso es el que pisan . . ." (I, 70) ("They go.— Vast, profound as the mysterious plateau of the world is the one they tread upon . . .").

The epigraph to part four, "La alborada" ("The dawn") (I, 71) is once again in Italian: "Già la terra è coperta d'uccisi; / Tutta è sangue la vasta pianura . . ." (I, 71) ("Now the earth is covered with slain men; the vast plain is all blood.") The source is a passage from the Italian Romantic Manzoni's *Il Conte di Carmagnola* descriptive of the battle of Maclodio.[29] In this part of his poem, Echeverría describes the attack of a group of horsemen on the Indian camp and the rescue of the remaining captives. Unfortunately Brian and María are not there.

The epigraph to part five, "El pajonal," "The scrubland" (I, 77) is again in Italian: ". . . e lo spirito lasso / Conforta, e ciba di speranza buona . . ." (". . . and comfort the weary spirit and feed on good hope . . .")

31

and from the eighth canto of Dante's *Divine Comedy*.[30] Now María tries to comfort and revive the wounded and exhausted Brian.

The epigraph to part six, "La espera," "The waiting" (I, 85) is from another Spanish playwright of the Golden Age, Moreto: ¡Qué largas son las horas del deseo!" ("How long are the hours of desire!").[31] In the play, *La confusión de un jardín (Confusion in a Garden)*, Don Luis, who has made his way to the garden of Doña Beatriz's home, hopeful of having an interview with her, makes this statement. It is psychologically true that circumstances have an effect on time; to María this period of waiting, filled with anxiety as she is, must seem an eternity. In the poet's words: ". . . ¡Cuán larga / Aquella noche y amarga / Sería a su corazón!" (I, 89) ". . . How long and bitter must that night have been to her heart!"

The epigraph to part seven, "La quemazón," "The pampas fire" (I, 91) is in French, from Lamartine's continuation of Byron's *Childe Harold*: "Voyez . . . Déjà la flamme en torrens se déploie." ("See . . . Already the flame spreads in torrents."[32] As originally used, the line marks the climax of a sea fight between Harold's men and the hostile Ottoman Turk; in the poem of Echeverría it anticipates the heroic rescue by María of her wounded Brian from the pampas fire.

The epigraph to part eight, "Brian," is a combination of two fragments from the Arabic poet Antar as rendered from an oral Italian version made by Lamartine's dragoman into French by the French Romantic poet, in reverse order from their appearance in the French publication used by Echeverría: "Les guerriers et les coursiers eux mêmes: Sont là pour attester les victoires de mon bras. / Je dois ma renommée à mon glaive . . ." (I, 101) ("The warriors and even the chargers themselves are there to attest to the victories of my arm. I owe my renown to my sword . . .)"[33] This section of the poem narrates the delirium and death of Brian; from his lips are heard reminiscences of his past deeds of courage as a warrior—these are foreshadowed by the passages drawn from Lamartine's "Fragments du Poème d'Antar." ("Fragments of Antar's Poem.") Antar was both poet and protagonist of a heroic poem.

The epigraphs to part nine, "María," are unusual in that they are two in number: the first one is anonymous: "Fallece esperanza y crece tormento." ("Hope dies and torment grows."); the second one is attributed properly to Petrarch, and Echeverría gives also a translation from Italian to Spanish: "Morte bella parea nel suo bel viso." ("Death appeared beautiful in her fair face") (I, 115). The Petrarchan passage is from his "Trionfo della Morte" ("Triumph of Death").[34] It has been impossible to locate the first and anonymous passage. In a letter, Roberto Giusti commented on various possibilities at some length; anything that Giusti has written on Echeverría is of interest; his remarks follow:

Cosa curiosa: ¿por qué el poeta no da el nombre del autor? Se me ocurre que porque tenía la conciencia de recordarlo vagamente, sin precisión: si el concepto, no los vocablos precisos. Otra singularidad: eso no es español. Lo sería 'fallece (la) esperanza, y (el) tormento crece." ¿Traducción de otra lengua que se autorizaba tales elipsis? En la famosa dedicatoria al conde de Lemos de los 'Trabajos de Persiles y Segismundo', tres días antes de morir Cervantes se despidió con una de las más conmovedoras páginas que hayan sido escritas. En ellas, como usted sabe, se lee: ' . . . el tiempo es breve, las ansias crecen, las esperanzas menguan . . . ,¿Serían estos sentimientos los que el poeta quiso poner, recordando por aproximación, acaso traduciendo, en su epígrafe? La interpretación se la ofrezco como conjetura.[35] (A curious thing: why doesn't the poet give the name of the author? It occurs to me that because he was conscious of recalling it vaguely, without precision: the idea but not the precise words. Another oddity: it's not Spanish. It would be so if it were written with the definite articles with the nouns. A translation from another language that permitted itself such ellipses? In the famous dedication to the Count of Lemos of the 'Labors of Persiles and Segismundo,' three days before dying, Cervantes took leave with one of the most moving pages that have been written. In them, as you know, one reads: ' . . . time is brief, anxieties grow, hopes decrease . . . ' Would these be the sentiments that the poet wished to put down, recalling approximately, perhaps translating, in his epigraph? I offer you the interpretation as a conjecture.)

The study of Echeverría presents a number of curious problems, and this one is one of them. Giusti was a teacher, critic, and admirer of Echeverría for many years, and his sympathy for Echeverría shines through his suggestions. Certainly, if the Cervantes passage was in Echeverría's mind, it would be appropriate to the description of María's death and transfiguration contained in this section of the poem.

The epigraph to part ten, an epilogue (I, 131), "Doux lumière, es-tu leur âme?" ("Sweet light, are you their souls?") is presented by Echeverría in French and in Spanish translation and prefaces his evocation of the lights that appear on high over the *ombú* tree, typical of Argentina's pampas, and may be the spirits or souls of María and of Brian. For Lamartine, the source of the epigraph, the *douce lumière*, or "sweet light," comes from an evening star; this light from the star may be the soul of someone who has passed away.[36]

Through this discussion of the epigraphs it has been possible to summarize the shifting scenes that make up *The Captive Woman*. It is as a succession of striking scenes that the poem has often been understood; this is the impression derived from Carlos M. Urien, who speaks of ". . . las impresiones que dominan al lector en las descripciones de 'La Cautiva': el desierto, el pajonal, la quemazón, el festín, la noche con sus bellezas, tristezas y espantosa lobreguez; cuadros que tanto llaman la atención por la robustez del colorido y las bellezas que su pluma traza a manera de pincel."[37] (". . . the impressions that dominate the reader in the descriptions of 'The Captive Woman': the desert, the scrubland, the pampas fire, the feast, the night with its beauties, sorrows, and frightful gloom; pictures which attract the attention so greatly by the strength of the coloring and the beauties that his pen traces in the manner of an artist's brush.")

V. The Poet's Purpose in Composing the Poem

Gutiérrez separated Echeverría's "Advertencia" or "Notice" to "The Captive Woman" from the poem, since it is in prose and also has individual value as a work of literary criticism which clarifies a poet's ideals about his own poetry. Evaluation of the poem, the one which is the chief basis of Echeverría's reputation as poet nowadays, cannot be fairly made without reference to this statement, which must be presented now (V, 143–149). Because of its length, use will be made of paraphrase of certain portions, and of our own translation, enclosed in quotation marks; space precludes presentation here of the Spanish text:

"The principal design of the author of *The Captive Woman* has been to depict some characteristics of the poetic face of the desert; and in order not to reduce his work to a mere description, he has placed, on the vast solitudes of the pampas, two ideal beings, or two souls united by the double bond of love and of misfortune. The event which he puts into poetry, if not certain, at least enters the realm of the possible; and since it is not for a poet to relate in minute detail all the circumstances like a chronicler or novelist, he has selected for building his portrait only those circumstances that might afford more local color to the brush of poetry: or, rather, he has scattered about the two figures that compose it some of the most characteristic ornaments of the surrounding nature. The Desert belongs to us, it is our richest patrimony, and we must try to derive from it not only wealth for our growth and well-being but also poetry for our moral delight and the encouragement of our national literature."

Echeverría goes on to explain that there are two dominant sides to the poem: externally, the energy of passion becomes manifest through actions, whereas internally, the struggle of this activity gradually consumes and, finally, annihilates like a lightning bolt its feeble existence. Intense passions are either satisfied when they are dissipated, or frustrated, in which case they also evaporate. The condition of being in the grip of strong passions is feverish and abnormal, not capable of being sustained, and the prelude to a crisis (V, 144).

"Purposely he uses colloquial expressions and names things by their name, because he thinks that poetry consists principally of ideas, and because not always, like them, do circumlocutions succeed in placing the object concretely before the reader's eyes. If this shocks those accustomed to high-sounding words and pompous ornamentation in poetry for the senses only, they will be at fault, for they are seeking not what is contained in the intent of the author, but rather what most pleases them."

Highly ornamental poetry, he continues, has its staunch advocates; this has given rise to the impression that poetry exaggerates and lies; poetry neither lies nor exaggerates. Only preachers like Brother Gerund (the hero of Padre Isla's novel of the eighteenth century in which excesses of church preachers are satirized) and soulless poets confuse tinsel and reverberation of words with eloquence and poetry. The poet only occasionally copies reality as it appears to view; since it is the basic principle of art to represent the beautiful, he must eliminate some of the blemishes. He takes what is natural or real just as the potter takes clay, the sculptor marble, the painter his colors, and then transforms them in accordance with his skill, into the likeness of the archetypes conceived by his mind. Nature and man give the poet primitive colors to be mixed and combined, sketches which he puts into relief, retouches, and gives character to impulses and ideas converted into models of intelligence and freedom, impressed with the most brilliant and elevated form capable of being conceived by the human mind. The true poet idealizes, replacing an imperfect reality with the likeness of a higher one (V, 145–146). "Physical and moral beauty, thus conceived, both in the ideas and affects of man and in his acts, both in God and in His magnificent creations—here lies the inexhaustible source of poetry, the principle and goal of Art, and the lofty sphere in which its marvelous creations move" (V, 146).

Echeverría then mentions poetry of a lower plane, humbler and more pedestrian, poetic only in employing verses and rhymes. Poetry of this type does not inspire and is as insipid as a fruit out of season (V, 156).

"Form, that is, the choice of meter, the exposition and structure of the "Captive Woman," are exclusively the author's; not recognizing any form normal in the mould of which artistic conceptions necessarily must be put, he has had to select the one that best suited the realization of his thought" (V, 147).

Echeverría goes on to say that the writer who mutilates his concept in order to fit it into a given mould is even less a poet than the one who imitates; artistic form is an integral part of the thought. Poetry has been classified by theorists who have not recognized this principle; they have classified poetry in the same way that mineralogists have classified crystals, by externals, and invented meaningless categories like *letrillas* or "poems in a light vein," eclogues, idylls, and the like, with divisions of genres into subdivisions. For them poetry is reduced to imitations and models; if the poet does not compose something recognized as fitting the pattern of one of these arbitrary classes, the gates of Parnassus are closed to him. Most Spanish poets have forced themselves into these classifications, wasting their talent without retaining any appeal in their work (V, 147–148).

"With regard to the octosyllabic meter in which this volume is written, he will say only that one day he fell in love with it in spite of the discredit to which writers of couplets had reduced it. It seemed to him one of the most beautiful and flexible of our language, and he tried to make it recover the luster which it enjoyed in the most flourishing periods of Castilian poetry, applying it to the expression of elevated ideas with deep feelings. He will have attained his purpose if the reader, upon reading through his *Rimas* (*Rhymes*) does not notice that he is reading octosyllables.

Meter, or better, rhythm, is the music by means of which poetry captivates the sentiments and works with most efficacy on the soul" (V, 148).

Here Echeverría repeats almost word for word the comments he made in his remarks on style, language, rhythm, and method of exposition, quoted in the discussion of *Elvira* (V, 119). Echeverría says: "There is, then, no complete poetry without rhythm. An instrument of art must in the poet's hands harmonize with his inspiration and adjust its measures to the various movement of the feelings. Hence rises the necessity of changing at times the meter in order to slow down or accelerate the voice, and give, as it were, to the song the intonations in accordance with the effect that is intended" (V, 148–149).

Echeverría concludes this notice, perhaps the most fruitful of his works of literary criticism, with a remark that two other poems, the "Himno al dolor" ("Hymn to suffering") and the "Versos al corazón" ("Verses to the heart") are of the same period as the *Consolations* and that the ideas expressed by them belong to humanity, even though they may seem to be expressions of an individual's feeling (V, 149).

Echeverría's comment on the use of the octosyllable in this poem may have misled critics; it should be read in relation to the need later expressed by him in the same notice for change in meter. In part two there are two stanzas with six-syllable lines; in part four, there are seven stanzas with lines of twelve and six syllables; in part seven, there are five stanzas with six-syllable lines. No part is without octosyllables, and this type of line is dominant. Assonance in *é-a* is found only in part two. There is one section in part two where use is made of lines of four syllables, the fight between Brian and the Indians—the four-syllable lines are devoted to Brian, his appearance in battle, his raising his sword to send rolling the heads of the Indians Quitur and Callupán, his facing the remaining Indians like an enraged bull, and then his fall, like a colt on the plain, felled by the *bolas*, that Indian instrument of the pampa used to bring cattle or horses to the ground (I, 51–52). It is worth focussing attention on parts of the poem with six (or twelve) syllable lines. The first one is the fight between Brian and the strongest of the pampa Indians, Chañil, told in sixteen lines (I, 53). This ends with Chañil's death, and Echeverría closes with the ambiguous exhortation: "Lloremos la muerte / Del indio más fuerte / Que la pampa crió." ("Let us bemoan the death of the strongest Indian that the pampa has reared") (I, 53). There may be some grim humor here, but the passage may also be interpreted as a tribute to strength in a redoubtable enemy.

The next variation in syllabic lines takes place in part four at the sudden attack by the Christians on the Indians, beginning with the alarm:

> Entonces, el grito, "Cristiano, Cristiano"
> Resuena en el llano.
> "Cristiano" repite confuso clamor,
> La turba que duerme despierta turbada,
> Clamando azorada,
> "Cristiano nos cerca, cristiano traidor" (I, 73).

("Then, the cry, 'Christian, Christian' resounds on the plain, 'Christian' repeats a confused clamor. The horde which sleeps wakes up disturbed, exclaiming in panic, 'Christian surrounds us, treacherous Christian.' ") The translation suggests that the Indians' Spanish here may be limited to key words, without the adornment of articles or qualifiers other than *traidor*, "treacherous." Here we have six-syllable lines separated by couplets of twelve-syllable lines.

Six-syllable lines are used also in part seven in the description of the pampas fire, to express the rapid, unexpected spread of the flames: "Raudal vomitando, / Venía de llama, / Que hirviendo, silbando, / Se encrosca Y derrama / Con velocidad" (I, 94). ("Vomiting a torrent, it came as a flame, that seething, hissing, coils up and spreads rapidly.")

It is clear that Echeverría reserved the changes in meter for moments of crisis, the arm-to-arm combat of Brian against individual Indians, the surprise attack by the Christians on the pagan Indians, the sudden appearance of the pampas fire which confronts María and Brian; María's reaction is brought into the stanza of which the first part has just been quoted: "Sentada María / Con su Brian la vía: / 'Dios mio! decía, / De nos ten piedad' " (I, 94). ("María, seated, could see it with her Brian: 'My God!' she said, 'Have pity on us!' ") This is, after all, the purpose of metrical variation, that the poet shifts the meter to accord with the changing action or mood of the narrative. The fact that other exciting moments in the poem, such as the raid and the feast, do not occasion the use of lines other than the octosyllable, shows that these variations are not applied mechanically by Echeverría, and that lines may be varied in length so as to accord with different emotions and needs.

VI. "The Captive Woman," A Rousing Success

There are external signs of the success of "The Captive Woman." It is significant that Domingo Faustino Sarmiento goes to its pages to illustrate his discussion of the fact that the Argentinian people are poetic by character, by nature. He asks the rhetorical question: "How can the person who witnesses these imposing scenes fail to be a poet?" And as depiction of the scenes quotes the second stanza of the first part of Echeverría's poem:

> Gira en vano, reconcentra
> Su inmensidad, y no encuentra
> La vista, en su vivo anhelo,
> Do fijar su fugaz vuelo,
> Como el pájaro en el mar.
> Do quier campos y heredades
> Del ave y bruto guaridas,
> Do quier cielo y soledades
> De Dios sólo conocidas,
> Que él sólo puede sondar.[38]

("The sight rotates in vain, compresses its immensity, and does not find

37

in its keen yearning any place wherein to fix its fleeting course, like the bird on the sea. Everywhere fields and estates, refuges of bird and beast, everywhere sky and solitudes known only by God, which only He can explore") (I, 36).

"The Captive Woman" is the chief poem in the volume called *Rimas (Rhymes)*, published in Buenos Aires in 1837. Two years later, in 1839, there was a Spanish edition, published in Cádiz, an unusual and clear mark of success.[39] The first part of the poem was translated literally into French to give an exact idea of the pampas by Jean Antoine Victor Martin de Moussy for inclusion in his *Description géographique et statistique de la Confédération Argentine* (V, xl). This French work was published in Paris in 1860.[40] "The Captive Woman" inspired the German painter of Latin America, Johann Moritz Rugendas, to illustrate its scenes.[41] The local color found in the poem is a matter of praise from Domingo Faustino Sarmiento, who found Walt Whitman, perhaps the epitome of the nineteenth century American spirit, "superior in style, but lacking in the local color which abounds in Echeverría's 'The Captive Woman.' "[42] It has been suggested that part of the reason for the success of Echeverría among the young intellectuals of Buenos Aires of the Literary Salon and the Association of May was his reputation as poet, a reputation crowned by "The Captive Woman," parts of which were read before the group by Juan María Gutiérrez. Ernesto Morales has related vividly the success of the *Rhymes* in the poet's day even in Buenos Aires where Echeverría's enemy, the despot Rosas, held sway. In 1845 a subscription was opened to pay for the publication of a pirated, unauthorized edition of the collection; the book came out in Buenos Aires from the José María Arzac printers in 1846.[43]

In 1861 a free translation of "The Captive Woman" was included in Karl Wilhelm Diehl's *Cisatlantisch*, a German version. Diehl used as pen name Wilhelm Walther, and entitled that part of his poem "In der Pampa" ("In the pampa").

In 1905 Charles W. Humphreys published an English version, "The Captive Woman," indicating that it was "to the enduring memory of the Argentine poet," and that it was a "slight tribute of admiration" from an Englishman. Since it was published in Buenos Aires, it is not readily available outside Argentina, but it is a faithful and readable translation with a biographical sketch. As example of Humphreys's success with the venture we quote the opening stanza—first the Spanish text, and then the English translation:

> Era la tarde, y la hora
> En que el sol la cresta dora
> De los Andes.—El Desierto
> Inconmensurable, abierto,
> Y misterioso a sus pies
> Se extiende—triste el semblante,
> Solitario y taciturno

Como el mar, cuando un instante
Al crepúsculo nocturno,
Pone rienda a su altivez (I, 35–36).
('Twas evening and the hour in which the sun
Upon the crest of Andes falls in gold.
The immeasurable desert at its feet
Lies hushed in mystery, as when twilight stills
the swelling of the sea . . .)[44]

Humphreys does not retain the rhyme and uses iambic pentameter here; like Echeverría, he varies his English meter. Some passages make use of rhyme. In the passage which narrates the death of Cheñil, for example, rhyme is apparent:

Like a colt upon the plain
Shall the body of the slain
Draw the vultures in its train.
Weep, weep ye for Cheñil!
Our bravest, with the steel
Of the long lance in his breast.
Well their onset he withstood!
With a funeral of blood
We have left him on the plain.
Not a white man did remain,
Our bravest and our best.[45]

In his credo, Echeverría pointed out the need for the poet to reflect the setting (the pampas), local manners and customs (the *malón* or Indian raid, the use of the horse, the use of the *bolas* would be concrete examples), and the inclusion of the ideas or thought of the time. One of the most important ideas of Echeverría and the young liberal thinkers in his circle was, of course, the concept of May, or of the independence of the nation. This is brought into the poem in the passage where Brian reviews his past days of glory, fighting under General San Martín, under the blue banner, just before his death (I, 111–113). Another of the most important of Hispanic concepts, living in the Romantics as well as in the Golden Age, is the idea of honor, the idea of unsullied feminine virtue, something a woman must live up to completely, no matter what the purity of the father, husband, brothers, or sons might be. This is brought out early in the poem when María reaches the side of the captured Brian. When he recognizes her, at first kissing and embracing her, he suddenly realizes the logical explanation of her presence with him there, that her honor has been stained by the lust of a savage Indian (I, 64–65). It is impossible for him to love her any more. This section of the poem has displeased some readers, but is in complete accord with the tradition of honor and with Romantic dramatic literature. A parallel, familiar to opera lovers who know Verdi's *Il trovatore (The Troubadour)*, is found in the source of that opera, the Spanish play *El trovador (The Troubadour)* of García Gutiérrez.

In the play, Leonor—having taken poison rather than permit the Count

to possess her—comes to the cell where her beloved Manrique is impris-
oned; she tells him that he is free; Manrique, with a perspective very similar
to that of Brian, assumes a horrible possibility, that Leonor had sold herself
to the Count, and he spurns freedom obtained at such a cost. In the depths
of despair he laments: "Ya no hay amor, / en el mundo no hay virtud."[46]
("No longer is there love, in the world there is no virtue.") The editors of
the play, realizing the differences between the Hispanic and American idea
of honor, comment specifically on this part of the play: "Notice the emphasis
laid upon the honor of women. Manrique typifies the real Spanish hero to
whom the honor of his betrothed is more sacred than life itself. No wonder,
then, that he prefers death when he finds his liberty to have been purchased
at the cost of a happiness which is dearer to him than his own life."[47] If for
Manrique, the name of Brian is substituted, for "betrothed," the word "María"
or "wife," for "finds," "assumes" or "thinks," the passage explicates the
situation in the "The Captive Woman." In both cases, it should be noted,
the audience or reader knows the truth better than the hero. When Brian
realizes the truth, he called her *mujer sublime* or "sublime woman" (I, 67)
just as Manrique is able to ask for his lute to tell of Leonor's virtue. In other
words, Echeverría's depiction here of what strikes an American reader as
eccentric behavior turns out to be a telling example of the way the Hispanic
hero is supposed to act to prove his *machismo* or "manliness," a concept
intimately related to that of honor. This attitude does not surprise María,
who does not react with hurt, outraged innocence, but rather, familiar as
she—Hispanic woman—is with the honor code, explains the circumstances
that permitted her to retain her purity and honor; she expresses the idea
romantically saying that powerful love gave to her the dagger in order to
kill any savage that insolently might attempt to outrage her honor, so that
she might avenge the death of her parents and young son (I, 65–66). To a
reader with other patterns of behavior this may seem strange, but it is not
strange for the honor code it exemplifies.

Faith in God on the part of the Christians of the poem is another aspect
of the life view of the civilized Argentinian of Echeverría's day. The female
captives silently raise their humble prayers to God (I, 54). God sends to
Brian and María a star to guide their flight by; María compares this star with
the red cloud seen by Israel, likewise sent by God (I, 69). When María gives
Brian water to drink to restore his energy, she expresses the idea that they
should courageously wait for the end implored by them from God (I, 83).
Interestingly, this action brings to mind the epigraph from Byron, and particularly the parallel between María and the woman of Samaria who left her
water jar after the conversation with Jesus told in the fourth book of the
gospel according to John. Not only does the poet himself enter the poem to
beseech God's permitting María's hope to see even one divine ray (I, 119).
Later he says, in similar vein, ". . . —¿Adónde / Tu poder ¡oh Dios! se
esconde? / Está por ventura exhausto? / Más dolor en holocausto / Pide a
una flaca mujer?" (I, 123) ("Where doth Thy power, oh God, hide? Is it
perchance exhausted? Does it ask of a frail woman for more grief in sac-

40

rifice?") The answer comes almost at once in the cry of the bird of the pampas, the *yajá* (or *chajá*), a term from the language of the Guaraní Indians of Paraguay and northern Argentina, applied to a type of wading bird of that area; this cry gives hope. The bird's name is derived from its cry, which has the meaning "let's go" in Guaraní. At its first appearance in the poem, Echeverría supplies an interesting note in which he refers to its significance as an alarm; it is nocturnal and repeats its call when it hears the noise of people approaching. People familiar with this characteristic of the bird prepare themselves for a possible attack from an enemy (I, 39). A sort of syncretism of genuine Christianity and traditional folk superstition, not infrequent in parts of the Americas, may be glimpsed in this passage.

A solitary cross, too, marks María's grave, shaded by the characteristic tree of the pampas, the *ombú* (I, 133–134). The birds nesting in the tree join in protecting the grave. There is some appeal to the supernatural, the mysterious appearance of two *luces* or "lights" at the spot where María is buried, the reaction of Indians who pass near, shouting "allí está la cruz." ("there lies the cross") (I, 135). Thereupon they turn their heads back as if fearful of seeing the angry, terrifying spectre of Brian. References to the bird called *yajá* and the ombú tree are merely two of the poem's localisms; there are such words as *toldería*, "group of wigwams of the Indians" (I, 36), *ranchos*, here equated with "straw cabins of the countryside" (I, 42), *huinca*, word used by the Indian to refer to the Christian or person of a different race, somewhat like the English "paleface" (I, 51), *Valichu*, the evil spirit of the pampas (I, 52).

Some of the negative criticism, particularly in recent years, valuable for showing flaws of the poem for the twentieth-century reader, can be used to show that Echeverría achieved his purpose well. It is his concept that may be viewed as flawed, rather than his ability to accomplish his goal. And flaws of this sort are quite possibly flaws for the moment, and may have been virtues in the past, and even, given the tendency for vogues in taste to change, again in the future. Americans who find interesting the narrative poems of Henry Wadsworth Longfellow should have little difficulty in regarding "The Captive Woman" as a meritorious work, even if they have not nationalistic or historical bias, as natives of Argentina might.

One critic has written: "The poem is not a literary masterpiece and is more of interest for what it tells us about Echeverría than for any intrinsic beauty. Certainly the contrast between the savage energy of Indian and nature and the passiveness and impotence of the white couple appears to reflect not the sturdy values of a pioneer civilization but the tired resignation of a dying race."[48] Masterpiece is a rather ambiguous term; it will be agreed that "The Captive Woman" does not have the scope of the Homeric poems or of Domingo Faustino Sarmiento's *Facundo*, but to deny it intrinsic beauty seems harsh. Nature and hostile Indians are powerful forces; if a reader recalls that Brian has been wounded—presumably his wounds are the cause of his death, rather than his passive impotence; and remembers his prowess in using his sword to make dread Indian warriors' heads roll, and that Echeverría has depicted in him a Romantic hero comparable in regard to the concept of honor with the hero of *El trovador*, he may not concur in this judgment. María, too, has been forced by circumstances to commit murder, to take a badly wounded and beloved husband away from his captivity and to set out over a hostile pampa; beset by pampas fire, afraid of discovery by the Indians (I, 78), attacked by the merciless heat of the summer sun (I, 79), she is able to carry her wounded husband on her back, and cross a swollen stream bearing her husband on the surface of the water (I, 97–98). The reader may recall that in the raid the Indians killed her parents as well as her son, as well as severely wounding her husband. How many readers of either sex, in the twentieth century, would not be silent if the sound of the *tigre*, "New World tiger or mountain lion," in search of prey, were in the vicinity? (I, 90). Even the dread *caudillo* Facundo found the *tigre* of Argentina a worthy foe, as related by Sarmiento in his masterly account of this rival of Rosas in barbaric qualities.[49]

If this critic senses savage energy in the Indian and passiveness and impotence in the whites, a reader may in challenge point to part four, where the Christians attack the Indians, not sparing woman, or man, or child of the tribe responsible for the abduction of Brian and María (I, 75). The female captives are moved to tears of joy at being saved by their husbands, and sons, but the rescuers are sad not to find Brian, his valor and his loyalty there (I, 73–74). Rather than showing savage energy in the Indian and resignation of a dying race in the white man, Echeverría shows that on both sides there is savagery. The special significance of the vengeance on the Indians and the rescue of all the captives except María and Brian is the irony of a fate that would permit the superhuman energy of María to rescue her husband, when, had she only waited, the rescue of both of them might have been effected and Brian might have recovered from the effects of his wounds. Fate, some might say, but Echeverría, a Romantic who had great admiration for women, attributed María's fate to love:

> El destino de tu vida
> Fue amar, amor tu delirio,
> Amor causó tu martirio,
> Te dio sobrehumano ser;
> Y amor, en edad florida,
> Sofocó la pasión tierna,
> Que omnipotencia de eterna
> Trajo consigo al nacer (I, 133).

("The destiny of your life was to love, love your delirium, love caused your martyrdom, giving you superhuman existence; and love, in the flower of your age, suffocated the tender passion, which with your birth brought with it the omnipotence of being eternal.")

Another critic feels that María is as manly as Brian.[50] It is true that Echeverría begins the epilogue of the poem with these words: "¡Oh María! Tu Heroísmo, / Tu varonil fortaleza, / Tu juventud y belleza / Merecieran fin mejor" (I, 131). ("Oh María! Your heroism, your manly strength, your youth and beauty had merited a better end.") But it is only her strength, under the stress of special circumstances, that earns the adjective *varonil*, "manly." The criticism has some point, but Brian was seriously wounded and María was motivated by the power of love to perform her superhuman, "manly" deeds. The masculine qualities of María are not emphasized in such passages as the following: ". . . ya no siente, / Ni llora, porque la fuente / Del sentimiento fecunda, / Que el feminil pecho inunda, / Consumió el voraz dolor" (I, 61–62). (". . . no longer does she feel, nor weep, because the abundant source of feelings which floods the feminine breast was consumed by voracious grief.") and ". . . silenciosa ella, / Como tímida doncella, / Besa su entreabierta boca . . ." (". . . silently she, like a timid maiden, kisses his half-open mouth") (I, 63). Echeverría answers his question as to what María would be without love by saying, "Frágil caña / Que el más leve impulso quiebra, / Ser delicado, fina hebra, / Sensible y flaca mujer" (I, 87). ("A fragile reed that the slightest impulse breaks, a delicate being, a fine thread, a sensitive, a frail woman.") But Love converts her into a divine being, a powerful and tender angel, whom Hell would not cause to waver, nor to tremble. None of this is appropriate, really, to Brian, as described by Echeverría—more than once the reader is told by the poet that it is the power of love that has given María this very special strength. In the discussion of Brian's energy, examples have been given of the poet's depiction of his manliness; actually critics seem to have been worried about María's womanliness less than about Brian's manliness. They have not recognized sufficiently the seriousness of his wounds, nor noted the clues given by the poet of his courage, strength, and heroic qualities.

One charge levelled against Echeverría's poem is that it is not an authentic expression of the pampa, inasmuch as the gaucho does not appear at all.[51] It is a temptation to answer the charge by appealing to Jorge Luis Borges's "conviction that one's expression of national or group identity need not, and should not, be deliberately set forth."[52] Borges cited with approval Gibbon's observation that in the *Koran* there are no camels, and stated in this connection: ". . . si hubiera alguna duda sobre la autenticidad del *Alcorán*, bastaría esta ausencia de camellos para probar que es árabe.[53] (". . . if there were some doubt about the authenticity of the *Koran*, this absence of camels would suffice to prove that it is Arabic.")

The gaucho, however, does appear in the poem by allusion: "Pero tú la tempestad, / Día y noche vigilante, / Anuncias al gaucho errante" (I, 123); ("But you announce to the wandering gaucho the storm, watching day and night.") Echeverría here is apostrophizing the *yajá* bird. It is true that no character is portrayed in the role of gaucho in the poem, but some gaucho characteristics appear. The barbaric, untutored quality of the gaucho is visible in the impious voice of the soldier who raucously announces to María that her son had been beheaded by the Indians (I, 125). Brian, too, in delirium shares the fondness of the gaucho for his horse and his weapon, when he calls for his horse and his lance (I, 108, 109).

Not necessary, but not inappropriate to the appreciation of the poem's value is the possibility that it be read for its parallels with the political and social situation of Argentina. María may symbolize Argentina, and the savages who murder her child may represent the barbarism of the pampa as exemplified by the cruelties of the despot Rosas. Brian, too, as a brave fighter in the War of Independence, can symbolize the spirit of May (Argentina's independence).[54]

Criticism directed against the portrayal of credible, individualized characters is inappropriate since Echeverría desired to depict idealized beings. It can only serve to explain lack of enthusiasm for reading the poem nowadays, since many modern readers expect psychologically convincing characterization. Psychology as a handmaid to literary criticism does not always lead to like views. There are opposed opinions about María's apparent inconsistency with regard to knowledge of the poet's part, or superior knowledge of the psychology of grief.[55] The latter interpretation may be defended, certainly, but hardly can be proved correct beyond doubt. The fact that such discussion is possible means that readers can take seriously the motives and actions of this "ideal(ized) being," and that Echeverría's narrative is not beyond the realm of what could have happened.

Professor Juan Collantes de Terán of the University of Seville has published the fullest literary discussion in recent years of "The Captive Woman," focussing attention on the first eleven stanzas of the first part of the poem.[56] To close the assessment of this poem, it is convenient to review his findings. Collantes de Terán finds perfection in the structuring of the poem through the predominance of a great expository unity.[57] He gives examples of the creation of tone or mood through attention to the time of day, the coloring and emotional setting of the landscape. His analysis finds that Echeverría's technique is in accord with the Romantic taste of his day, new at the time.[58] "The Captive Woman" displays the exaltation of the feelings characteristic of Romanticism, the sensations associated with the coming of night, for example, with its accompanying sorrow, the effect of the moods of Nature on the feelings of the poet; solitude intensifies sorrow. Collantes de Terán quotes the passage that Sarmiento includes in *Facundo* as an example of the distance separating the Romantic writer, where the attitude of the author is made clear, from the vision afforded by the Classical one.[59]

He also notes the avoidance of specific exaltation of freedom in these pages, which must be deduced from scrutiny of the title with its symbolic possibilities and from the figures employed and details of the language rather than from anything overt. If the attempt is made to apply knowledge of the poet's life as an exile in Montevideo, and allow that to shed light on his feeling toward the pampa or "desert" of his native land, two risks exist; Echeverría's exile began a few years after his publication of the poem, and a work of art need not be a photographic representation of the writer's individual biography.

Echeverría is seen to be a careful user of appropriate color-terms, particularly those related to black, darkness, yellow, brown, blue, green, with a view to intensifying emotion.[60] Echeverría exemplifies the philosophical opposition of reason against feelings or emotions.[61] Collantes de Terán also finds in "The Captive Woman" an innovation—its closeness to the sketch of manners, or the form of writing of the *costumbristas*, those who write on customs.[62] As a specific example, he refers to the presence of the word *toldería* applied to the Indian dwellings, "wigwams" for the North American, made of wood and hide; attention to this sort of detail, Collantes de Terán feels, is significant in appearing during the first half of the nineteenth century, the historical moment in which the writers on manners and customs dedicated their attention to careful observation of the milieu.[63] Another example is the reference to the *yajá* bird.[64] Lastly, Collantes de Terán finds worthy of esteem Echeverría's versification, his use of eight-syllable lines in "The Captive Woman," siding with critics like Emilio Carilla and against those like Enrique Anderson Imbert and Rafael Alberto Arrieta.[65] When experts in literary criticism and history, native speakers of Spanish, disagree, the most that an outsider can do is state that Echeverría's versification is successful enough to win praise from some, if not all, qualified critics.

All in all, the continued popularity of "The Captive Woman," frequently reprinted, as a true, albeit minor, masterpiece seems fully justified; for the student of Romanticism in Argentina and in Spanish America or for the reader of Echeverría, it is full of interest.

VII. Echeverría Versifies Current Revolutionary History

The problem the poet next set for himself was a very different one. Now he was to celebrate a recent event in the history of Argentina. The poem *Insurrección del Sur (Insurrection of the South)* is dated November, 1839 at Echeverría's country estate in Los Talas; it was not published until 1849 in Montevideo. Instead of ideal beings in the setting of the pampa, the actors are historic. The work is dedicated to the memory of Pedro Castelli (1796–1839),[66] Ambrosio Crámer (1792–1839),[67] Manuel Leoncio Rico (1798–1841),[68] Domingo Lastra (1795–1839),[69] Matías Ramos Mejía (1810–1885),[70] and other patriots, most of whom died at the battle of Chascomús on November 7, 1839 and all of whom participated in the insurrection which took place from October of that year in the southern part of the province of Buenos Aires. How was Echeverría to compose a narrative poem on recent events in which he would deal with people known to many of his potential readers? Such a poem would necessarily mean openly attacking the dictator Rosas, against whom the insurrection was directed. The events, too, would be well known, so that there would be little or no suspense from the course of events. Since Echeverría's purpose was to honor the memory of these men, as well as to display the power of the pen against Rosas, panegyric, propaganda, and history would have to be part of the work. Echeverría would not be in the position of a Vergil or a Camoëns, celebrating events not directly contemporary; he would be in a position more like that of a modern newspaper correspondent, but he would have the disadvantage of knowing that what he wrote would make it impossible for him to continue to live in Argentina unless somehow Rosas were overthrown or killed.

Criticism has been almost unanimous in the opinion that the faithfulness to history makes it a less than successful poem. One critic, however, has given a sympathetic evaluation, which emphasizes its appeal for a reader in Argentina, hostile to tyranny, and familiar with national history. According to Palacios, the hero of the poem is the gaucho, particularly the gaucho who revolted in the countryside of the southern part of the province of Buenos Aires where Rosas had reason to believe himself surpreme; this was the region where Rosas developed his early political strength. Its leader, Pedro Castelli, was the son of one of the participants of the birth of independence in May of 1810.[71]

Technically, *Insurrection of the South*, shows the variety of meter of the other narrative poems. The use of ballad-type meter, however, is restricted to part five of the poem, which deals with the unexpected betrayal and defeat of the rebel forces at the battle of Chascomús. In this section of the poem, too, occur some of the best examples of local color, the description of Chascomús near the famed lagoon of the same name (I, 245–246), the joyous trampling underfoot the emblem of tyrant Rosas and unfurling the blue colors of May (I, 245–247), the gauchos making use of their lassoes, smoking, drinking *mate* or Paraguayan tea, grouped in circles around their fires (I, 247–248); the riflemen wearing cap, vest, and *chiripá* (the blanket-like trousers of the gaucho) (I, 251), a group of Indians with their *ponchos* (I, 252), the last-mentioned two groups representing the troops loyal to Rosas, as the rebel leaders, Castelli and Crámer, suddenly discover when they shout: "'Traición! traición, compañeros!/ Siervos son del vil tirano: / Viva la patria!—a la carga: / Vencer o morir matando" (I, 253). ("Treachery! treachery, companions! They are slaves of the base tyrant: long live the homeland!—charge; win or die killing.")

The poem is divided into nine parts: 1) Exhortation to weep for the heroic freedom-fighters and to continue to fight against the Minotaur, Rosas, for the values of May; 2) An appeal to the five thousand patriots, joined in fraternity, to continue the mission of May and overthrow the tyrant; 3) Buenos Aires hopes for the rebels' victory under Castelli; Echeverría taunts the coward despot, Rosas. 4) The patriots await reinforcements at Chascomús. 5) The rebels are confronted by treachery at Chascomús. 6) The course of the battle and defeat of the rebels are described. 7) The death penalty is decreed for the patriots; Rosas's fall is promised. 8) Echeverría castigates Rosas's legislators or representatives for "legalizing" the executions of the defeated rebels; Dolores meets a similar fate to that of Chascomús. 9) The uprising in Corrientes has also been suppressed; survivors take refuge, some of them in exile.

Annotation of the poem makes it of value as a historical document. Echeverría provides twenty-three notes, giving details as to the events which took place, identifying people, explaining regionalisms, and including the note written by the general of the forces of Rosas who were victorious in the battle to the Justice of Peace and military commander of Dolores, Don Mariano Ramírez. The general was younger brother of the tyrant, Rosas, named Prudencio Ortiz de Rozas (1800–1857). [72] The note was sent to accompany the head of Pedro Castelli, to be placed in the town square for public view, on a high pole, well secured so as not to be in danger of falling down (I, 278). Echeverría comments briefly: "Parece el rugido de un estúpido caníbal" (I, 278). ("It seems to be the roaring of a stupid cannibal.") Perhaps the most effective invective comes in the eighth part of the poem, when Echeverría attacks the legislators who approved the death penalty and the beheading of Castelli. For Echeverría these representatives of Rosas acted purely to make legal the deaths of the conquered; he points out that the rebels violated no law; those who violated and betrayed the people were those who sold and sacrificed the homeland to the tyrant. Traitors would be those who put the life and property of the citizens at the mercy of Rosas's whims (I, 276–277). Echeverría's point of view was similar to that expressed in the Declaration of Independence of the United States of America adopted by Congress on July 4, 1776: "A Prince, whose character is . . . marked by every act which may define a Tyrant, is unfit to be the ruler of a free people."[73] In Argentina's case the Prince or Tyrant was Rosas, so-called Restorer of the Laws. Echeverría warns these legislators that perhaps Rosas will turn on them: "Quizá vuestro amo un día, / Generoso y leal y justiciero, / Sonriendo con satánica ironía, / Por diversión os saque o fantasía / Para enviaros también al Matadero" (I, 269). ("Perhaps your master one day, generous and loyal and just, smiling with Satanic irony, for amusement will take you, or to suit his fancy, to send you too to the Slaughterhouse.") This reference to the Slaughterhouse, where Rosas's enemies are killed, may not be exactly like the poet's conception of Rosas's Federation being allegorically a slaughterhouse, but in any case the equation of Rosas and butcher can be drawn.

VIII. Current History Again—Marco María de Avellaneda

Insurrection of the South foreshadows the poem that takes its name from that of its hero, the martyr of Metán, Marco Avellaneda. The poem was dedicated to a friend of the poet from Tucumán, Juan Bautista Alberdi.[74] Its theme is like that of the earlier poem: rebellion against the tyranny of Rosas. Much of the earlier poem was completed in 1839, before Echeverría's flight to exile in Uruguay (I, 229–230). Both poems were published at about the same time, in 1849 and 1850.

In 1875, an Italian version of *Avellaneda* by Erminio Bettinotti was published in Buenos Aires.

Avellaneda contains a famous description of Tucumán, the birthplace of the poem's protagonist; some of Tucumán's heroes in the fight for independence or liberty are mentioned, as well as the effect of war on the city. Avellaneda's ideas and hopes form part of the narrative; the poem relates a vision he has urging him to emulate the past heroes and then details events of the unsuccessful revolution. The poem includes scenes—some of them in dialogue form—which present Marco at home with father, wife (Dolores),and their children. Eventually General Juan Lavalle is defeated, as is Avellaneda, at the Famaillá river. The leader of Rosas's forces is General Manuel Oribe; Avellaneda—through the treachery of his fellow fugitive after their defeat, Gregorio Sandoval—is captured, interrogated, and beheaded.

There is no doubt that the poem represents a mature mind; it is more varied in its appeal than its predecessor—the figure of Castelli is viewed almost totally as a revolutionary leader, whereas in *Avellaneda* the thinker and the family man are depicted. People have seen a bit of Echeverría's own attitudes in Avellaneda, but in any case it is a flesh and blood portrait of a real human being that is essayed. It has been characterized as his best narrative poem.[75] Among the parts of the poem that have been taken to reveal the views of Echeverría is the reference to the situation at the University of Buenos Aires when, beginning in 1821, sensualist philosophy and the principles of utilitarianism were taught (I, 437). Avellaneda tells his father that he has been a believer in Christianity for a short time, that his professors taught him to have doubts concerning God, virtue, heroism, good, justice, and himself (I, 340). Gutiérrez has commented on this passage and Echeverría's own annotation, explaining that the professors were seeking to emancipate the students, to make them apply reason to philosophical problems, and points out that the teaching bore good fruit in producing men like Echeverría, himself, and Avellaneda, who opposed Rosas's regime (I, 438).

Criticism of Rosas on the part of Avellaneda's father is expressed clearly and almost without emotion: "Rosas de las conciencias ha borrado / Las nociones morales / De derecho y deber, justicia y orden, / Y en la masa del pueblo inoculado / El principio del mal y del desorden" (I, 337). ("Rosas has erased from consciences the moral notions of law and duty, justice and order, and inoculated in the mass of the people the principle of evil and of disorder.") The restraint of this passage contrasts in tone with the more ardent statements of Marco.

Continuity between earlier patriots and Marco is maintained. Early in the poem the great men from Tucumán are presented: General Manuel Belgrano, a key figure in the struggle for independence,[76] and Bernardo Monteagudo, who took part in the May revolution of 1810.[77] Thus the spirit of May is made specific through these figures. The impact of their ideas is suggested by reference to the fiery lawyer, Mariano Moreno, and his translation of Rousseau's *Social Contract*, with the prophetic words: "Será tal vez nuestra suerte mudar de tiranos, sin destruir la tiranía" (I, 302, 435). ("It will perhaps be our fate the change tyrants, without destroying tyranny.") Rosas, indeed, replaced Spain.

This theme is reinforced by the appearance as in a dream to young Marco of the shades of Belgrano, Monteagudo, and General Antonio González Balcarce, hero of the battle of Suipacha of November 7, 1810.[78]

The most famous passage of *Avellaneda* occurs at the beginning, wherein Echeverría pays tribute, by imitation, to two of his favorite authors: Lord Byron and Goethe. The passage begins: "¿Conocéis esa tierra bendecida / Por la fecunda mano del Creador . . ." (I, 283) ("Do you know that land blessed by the Creator's fecund hand . . .") Here is a characteristic way of incorporating knowledge of Romantic poets in a new and American work. One student of Byron's influence on Echeverría has found the source in the first canto of Byron's "The Bride of Abydos."[79] As a matter of fact, the description fuses elements of the Byron poem with others from Goethe's "Kennst du das Land . . . [80] ("Knowest thou the land . . .") These he combines with the new setting. Echeverría's "orange trees" and "laurel" correspond exactly to Goethe's "gold oranges" and "laurel." On the other hand, Byron's "myrtle" and "cedar" are taken over by Echeverría in his *mirtos* and *cedro* (I, 284). But Echeverría adds *el camote*, "the sweet potato," *la rica chirimoya*, "the delicious custard apple," and the *pacará tree*, typical of Tucumán (I, 431). The study of influences on Echeverría has dangers; Roberto F. Giusti has expressed this clearly: "Señalar influencias en Echeverría, tan permeable a ellas, es fácil, pero difícil precisarlas, porque se entrecruzan en su obra."[81] ("To indicate influences in Echeverría, so susceptible to them, is easy, but it is difficult to pinpoint them, because they cross with each other in his work.")

There is vigor in the passages motivated by hate for Rosas and blood-thirsty General Oribe, concentrated in two fine lines addressed to the latter: "Las orejas en sal del traidor Borda / Manda en ofrenda a tu ídolo sangriento" (I, 381). ("Send as an offering to your blood-stained idol the ears of traitor Borda in salt.") The "idol" is Rosas.

The description of Tucumán finds an echo towards the poem's close, when the scene is repeated with variations, a sort of lull before the storm (I, 420–421). The scene of the decapitation of Avellaneda is suitably horrifying, and yet includes a simile of the Vergilian type, wherein the executioner's slicing of the throat of Avellaneda is compared with the woodsman's felling a tree with an axe (I, 429). In a note, Echeverría informs the reader that General Oribe had the corpse quartered, skinned, and hung in the trees next to the camp of Metán; then the skin was made into rods, and a whip which was sent as a gift to Rosas. The residents of Tucumán were required to stop and gaze at the head of Avellaneda on display in the main square. Those who were reluctant were whipped with the rods made out of the skin, together with shouts of laughter that the rod used was made of their Governor's hide" (I, 444). Avellaneda had been made governor of Tucumán in May of 1841 so that the taunt was appropriate in the mouths of Oribe's soldiers.

Even without the propaganda of the notes, the poem is an effective anti-Rosas document. Its scope is greater than that of "Insurrection of the South." In a letter to Alberdi, to whom the poem was dedicated, Echeverría has given a clue to his characterization of the protagonist. Echeverría expresses the idea that it is not possible to put contemporary events and characters into poetry, since poetry lives on idealization. Thus he has had to idealize Avellaneda by transforming the man that is depicted in all his poems, at different ages of life and in different situations.[82] This statement has been related to another in which Echeverría said that the Avellaneda of the poem was a "transformation" of the main character of *La guitarra (The Guitar)* and *El angel caído (The Fallen Angel)*.[83]

IX. The Opening of a Trilogy—The Guitar

The full title of *The Guitar* is *La guitarra o primera página de un libro (The Guitar or First Page of a Book)*. It has an epigraph on the title page from *The Tempest* (I, 137). The first part is from the exchange of comments between Alonso, king of Naples, and Gonzalo upon hearing "solemn and strange music."[84] Then come two lines from the reaction of Ferdinand to Ariel's famous "Full fathom five thy father lies . . ."[85] This double epigraph gives the clue to the harmony and sweetness of the music, and also to the appearance of mystery and even the supernatural (I, 136).

The Guitar was not published until 1849, though it has been suggested that it was written between 1840 and 1842.[86] Very roughly, it may be read as an autobiographical, idealized account in veiled terms of an episode in the poet's life before he left Buenos Aires for Paris, which led to a scandal, an ill-fated love affair.

It resembles earlier poems in having an epigraph, and differs from *Insurrection of the South* and *Avellaneda* in not being overtly historical or openly anti-Rosas. There is a hint of political attitude in the anticipatory look forward to the protagonist's return from Europe to offer his country his love and tribute, only to find it "agonizar entre las manos / De imbéciles y bárbaros tiranos . . ." (I, 225) ("agonizing amid the hands of imbeciles and barbarous tyrants"). The word *imbéciles* might be an adjective as well as a noun.

There are several strains in the poem, which has a very slight plot. Ramiro falls in love with young Celia, who is married to an older man she does not love. Music draws them together; Celia falls in love but does not betray her duty to her husband, who learns of the situation by hearing words uttered by his wife in her sleep. He tries to avenge his honor by fighting with Ramiro; a second fight is fatal to the husband, and results in a remorseful Ramiro's decision to give up his frivolous life and to be ruled by reason. Besides the motifs of the guitar (both Ramiro and Celia are accomplished players), the jealousy and the words overheard in a dream, there is the mysterious breaking of the strings of a guitar at crucial moments of the narrative.

The poem has been referred to as *Celia*, after the name of its heroine. It includes details of the Buenos Aires scene and the River Plate: the pampa breezes perfuming the area near the great river (I, 140), the guitar serenade at the *reja* or grill-worked window at Celia's home (I, 146), a country estate described (I, 148), the beauty of the port women or *porteñas* as the Buenos Aires women are called (I, 149), Barracas street with its estates (I, 181), changing taste in furniture (I, 190), a superstition about the will-o'-the-wisp, felt to be the soul in torment or that of a person killed without confession (I, 192–193). Ramiro is eighteen years old, like Celia, so that if the poem is thought of as autobiographical, it should depict scenes of 1823 or 1824. Caution in this regard, however, is desirable.

The mysterious vibration, and breaking, of the strings of the guitar at moments of crisis is a device attacked by critics.[87] It may be the result of European influence.

There is a tale by Theodor Körner entitled "Die Harfe" ("The Harp").[88] This story, written in the early years of the nineteenth century—Körner lived from 1791 to 1813—was put into verse under the title "Las nueve" ("Nine o'clock") by the Spanish Romantic poet, Father Juan Arolas, and published in Valencia in 1843.[89] Other works may include a similar detail, but the fact that Echeverría was making use of a device used by other writers, admittedly of a harp rather than of a guitar, makes it tempting to see an influence, either of Arolas or of Körner. "The Harp" tells of the sounding of the harp's strings after the death of the young wife of the tale and poem, who used to play, when alive, duets with her husband, a flautist. The strings break with his death. By 1846, Echeverría certainly was acquainted with works by Arolas, since he speaks of him as a poet who emphasizes form, unlike Byron, who can electrify the heart (II, 547). The kinship is certainly evident, but may be accidental.

The most serious charge made is that of plagiarism.[90] It is claimed that the episode in which Celia reveals her love to her husband as she sleeps is stolen from Byron's "Parisina."[91] Other parallels, too, between "Parisina" and *The Guitar* have been found.[92] There is an important difference between Byron's episode and Echeverría's: Celia's love for Ramiro does not involve physical misconduct. Bryon's heroine is guilty of illicit love in act as well as in heart.

Echeverría may have been inspired, also, by a real-life experience; people have been known to talk in their sleep. In addition, the dream episode has elements of Rossini's *Otello*. In the opera the heroine is guiltless; Echeverría knew both the Shakespeare play and the Rossini opera.[93]

In the play, Iago tells Othello that Cassio had dreamt that he was making love to Desdemona.[94] Rossini's opera, however, has another use of the dream motif. When Otello enters the bedroom bent on killing Desdemona, he hears her murmur: "My beloved!"[95] He wonders whom she is addressing, and whether she is dreaming or awake. Celia's husband, too, has doubts: "— ¿Quién será, cielos?—" (I, 153) ("Who can it be, by Heaven?")

Echeverría was fond of music and it is possible that Rossini's opera as well as Byron's poem was in his mind. There also may be echoes from Shakespeare's play in the dialogue between Celia and her husband.[96] He comments on her pallor and the fact that her eyes have traces of tears. She says that she sees something sinister in her husband's eyes and says that if

51

she wept, it was because of him. Then she asks him to listen to a song, which, with its guitar accompaniment, calms his jealousy (I, 161–162).

All in all, *The Guitar* remains readable and possesses interest for its autobiographical touches, glimpses of aspects of urban and suburban Buenos Aires life, its sincere depiction of unhappy love, its blending of music (the songs, the guitar, perhaps even allusions to opera), its maturity of versification.

X. The Fallen Angel—Echeverría's Proudest Work

Fragments of letters dated at Montevideo in January, 1844 and June, 1846, give Echeverría's concept of the poem. He recognizes that it will provoke varied criticism (II, 5). Its hero is a Don Juan, in whom are made concrete the good and bad qualities of men of his time and the poet's ideal dreams and hopes for the future, an American Proteus with many shapes. Angela, the heroine, who is the "fallen angel," is a fusion of social elements of the Argentinian woman of the day.

Customs, local color, pleasures and sorrows, hopes and disappointments, idealism and materialism, spirit and flesh—these are the elements that Echeverría seeks to display (II, 5–6).

The Fallen Angel is a continuation of *The Guitar*; pages corresponding to a European trip between the events of the two poems are omitted; the series was to have a sequel in the poem called *Pandemonium*. The three works together are envisaged as a vast epico-dramatic picture depicting individual and social life. The poet also hoped to make another excursion into the countryside as a sort of poetic appendix to "The Captive Woman."

It is unfortunate that the eminent Spanish scholar, Marcelino Menéndez y Pelayo, should have damned *The Fallen Angel* in witty but unsympathetic terms. According to him, much more than of Lamartine's *La Chute d'un ange (The Fall of an Angel)* could it be said of Echeverría's poem that it represents the fall of a poet, rather than that of an angel.[97] Menéndez y Pelayo felt that Echeverría's Don Juan was nobody because the poet insisted on making him everything.

In the course of the poem Echeverría clarifies his Don Juan; he is not the atheistic noble of Seville depicted by Tirso de Molina, Mozart, or others (II, 70). He is a son of the river Plate, influenced by the sun of May (II, 71). He is an idealist, searching for some unknown woman to absorb his ego (II, 145). His inspiration seems to have stemmed from Byron's *Don Juan*, Espronceda's *El estudiante de Salamanca (The Student of Salamanca)*, and Goethe's *Faust*.[98] References here are to the version of the complete works. There is another, in manuscript, found in the national archives, with passages not in the published edition.[99] Echeverría has discussed treatments before him in a brief, perhaps incomplete, essay, "La leyenda de Don Juan," ("The Legend of Don Juan.") He thinks the Spanish versions less profound than those of Byron or Mozart (V, 410–412).

It is useful to summarize the findings of a student of Byron's influence on Echeverría in *The Fallen Angel*; Posey's pages reflect careful study of the poem and are valuable.[100] He names the three main characters: Don Juan and Angela, whose functions are those stated in Echeverría's letter of January, 1844, and Don Luis, "idealist and a dreamer of unlimited capacity and unknown ability who has within him potentialities of which his social environment takes no heed."[101] *The Fallen Angel* is a work of protest and a satire. It is earnest; its drama is internal rather than external.[102] Echeverría's Don Juan is more patriotic than Byron's and is a mystic, Faust-like in his striving for the "supreme good." Woman is "the divine power which draws out the best that is in men and inspires them with a breath of the divine."[103] Don Juan is a good example of the Byronic hero. There is an essential difference between Byron's heroines and those of Echeverría. For Byron, a heroine "craves to love because that is the way she is made." But for Echeverría, the heroines have passions that are pure and divine, as well as natural. Digression is a feature of both poems. Posey recognizes that Echeverría, in adapting materials from Byron's *Don Juan* with the impress of the character of Buenos Aires, succeeded in creating a work that would have freshness for his contemporaries.[104] He provides well chosen parallel passages that show the imprint of Byron on Echeverría's most ambitious work.

Plot in *The Fallen Angel* is unimportant; the work is best considered as an evocation of scenes and incidents, interesting in themselves rather than as segments of a sequential chain. There are eleven parts, each one with a title: 1.) Don Juan a una niña en su día. (Don Juan to a girl on her (birth)day); 2.) El baile. (The dance.); 3.) Don Juan; 4.) Lances y percances. (Incidents and mishaps.); 5.) Amor en alba y ocaso. (Love at dawn and sunset.); 6.) Veinte años (Twenty years); 7.) Una noche (One night); 8.) Visiones (Visions); 9.) Otra noche (Another night); 10.) Revelación (Revelation); 11.) La glorieta del amor (The bower of Love). The girl of the first part, Angela, who has just lost her innocence, is twenty years old in the sixth part of the poem. In the final part of the poem, after the death of the Brazilian Pereira, Angela's husband, killed by Don Juan, the widow seeks in vain her real beloved. He has fled because of his criminal action in killing her husband (II, 526–527). This is perhaps enough to orient a reader, but it must be emphasized that individual episodes may have little to do with the work as a whole, though they do suit Echeverría's purpose in depicting the Buenos Aires in the years from 1830 on.

Echeverría makes use of reminiscence. For example, his former loves file past Don Juan in a sort of vision: Ada, Eloa, and Josefina of the river Seine, reflecting the Paris days (1825–1830) (II, 395–397); Ema of the Thames, from England in 1829 (II, 395–397); Deidalia from Italy (II, 397–398) whose counterpart is vague; Ramona, who first taught Don Juan to love (it is uncertain how literally to take this catalogue as corresponding to episodes in the poet's life) (II, 398). Ramona tells Don Juan that she has sought him for fifteen years,—in chronological terms from about 1823 to 1838, if it is desirable to fit the poem to the poet's life. This is followed by a clear reference to Celia of *The Guitar*, mad, with flowers in her hand like Shakespeare's Ophelia, pursued by the flashing eye of a fleshless, furious spectre, with dagger in his right hand, and another (Ramiro's) nailed in his chest, promising to pursue Ramiro (or Don Juan, or Echeverría, possibly) to Hell itself (II, 399). Estela follows (II, 399) and a circle has been made, since she is described as his new love in the fourth part (II, 158–160. This succession of loves makes appropriate the use of the name Don Juan; in view of the position of *The Fallen Angel* as sequel to *The Guitar*, the name Ramiro might still be usable.

One incident of the poem seems like history, but is hard to situate. Echeverría's heroine, Angela, is a member of the audience at a performance of a French play by Alexandre Dumas *père* entitled *Angèle* (*Angela* in Spanish). Young men in the audience comment on the fact that the name of the play's heroine is also the name of the most beautiful woman in the audience (II, 185). The scene is described wherein Dumas's Anjela (to use Echeverría's spelling) feels her sin and reveals her qualms to her lover, Alfred or Alfredo. He tries to comfort her, and she exclaims: "Dices bien, la mujer dicha regala / Y recoge vergüenza." (II, 195) ("You are right, woman gives happiness and receives shame.") His reply is: "Vergüenza, Angela, no ¿quién sabrá nunca / Si hay un secreto que nuestra alma esconde?" (II, 195). ("Shame, Angela, no. Who will ever know if there is a secret our souls hide?") Only public knowledge can be the source of shame, Alfredo implies. It is possible to identify exactly this scene and even the French text.[105] At this point in the performance, many glances looked toward the balcony where Angela and her mother were seated; the stain on her honor seemed to be public knowledge. Commotion ensues as the curtain falls.

Autobiographical elements in the poem suggest that an examination of the repertory of plays performed in Buenos Aires is in order. From Castagnino it is certain that there was a performance of this play at the Teatro de la Victoria in Buenos Aires on July 2, 1844.[106] The theater had been opened on May 24, 1838.[107] The first Dumas *père* play performed in Buenos Aires was *Antonino* in 1834.[108] In 1838, *La torre de Nesle* and *Catalina Howard* of the same playwright were performed, as well as García Gutiérrez's Spanish play, *El trovador*.[109] Just as *The Guitar* corresponds roughly to Echeverría's experience between 1823 and 1825, *The Fallen Angel* seems to depict the Buenos Aires of the years between 1830 and 1840. If such an incident actually took place in a Buenos Aires theater, Echeverría must have learned of it through hearsay. The play dates from 1833; the poet could have considered the potential drama of the scene, and created it from the imagination. Idealization might blur chronology; performance in Montevideo cannot be excluded.

Professor Castagnino, the authority on the stage in Buenos Aires during the Rosas era, dealt with some of these questions in a gracious letter; relevant comments follow: ". . . las respuestas que involucran la cuestión de

'El ángel caído,' sólo pueden ser dadas a título conjetural y debiendo admitir que lo autobiográfico de un poema no es, ineludiblemente, de rigor documental. A las hipótesis que usted formula, cabe agregar otras: movilidad de los elencos entre Montevideo y Buenos Aires; el que Echeverría supiera que la obra estaba en el repertorio, aunque no la representasen; el conocimiento, por lectura del texto; la familiaridad con los medios teatrales de ambas orillas del Plata. Consiguientemente, inducir que Echeverría imagina como sucedidos pormenores de una función, etc."[110] (". . . the answers that relate to the problem of *The Fallen Angel* can only be given in a conjectural way and with the need of admitting that the autobiographical part of a poem is not, unavoidably, of documental rigor. To the hypotheses formulated by you should be added others: the mobility of the casts between Montevideo and Buenos Aires; the fact that Echeverría might know that the work was in the repertory, although it was not performed; knowledge, through reading of the text; familiarity with the theatrical milieus on both shores of the river Plate . . . Consequently, to deduce that Echeverría imagines as having taken place details of a performance, etc.")

A clearer example of chronological license is presented by Echeverría's song, "El desamor" ("Indifference"). It appeared in *Rhymes* in 1837 (III, 180–182). It forms a part of *The Guitar*, which seems to be set in Echeverría's pre-Paris period (I, 180–182). "Indifference" was set to music by Juan Pedro Esnaola in 1836.[111] Collaboration with Esnaola did not take place until about this time.

Esnaola is referred to in *The Fallen Angel* when the heroine, Angela, announces that she will sing a song composed by Esnaola to words by some unknown Argentinian (II, 338–339). It begins: "Amor es armonía / De inefable pureza, / Amor es alegría / Sin nube de pesar" (II, 291); ("Love is harmony of ineffable purity, love is joy without a cloud of unhappiness";). This song is not found as a separate composition of Echeverría, yet the reference suggests that he is the author of the text. Since Angela is twenty at the time, 1835 suggests itself as the date of her singing the selection.

These examples afford insight into the fascinating problems caused by Echeverría's technique of idealizing or of placing his ideal self in a variety of situations. The atmosphere is evoked specifically enough to make these events probable.

Another much praised passage is Don Juan's apostrophe to the river Plate[112] (II, 223–230). The desire for oblivion is movingly expressed, especially because the resting place of Echeverría's remains is not known: ". . . Para que no viese el hombre / Sobre Lápida ninguna / Jamás escrito mi nombre / Ni preguntase quién fue" (II, 229–230). (". . . so that no man might see on any tombstone ever written my name nor ask who it was.") The description of the dance is a very successful section.[113] One interesting feature is the use of a repeated refrain of seven lines like background music in a film, interrupting passages of dialogue, some of which may be assumed as taking place simultaneously. This refrain begins: "La música en tanto sonora vertía / Su rica armonía / Por la vasta sala, bañada en fulgor" (II,

96, 102, 108, 112). ("The music meanwhile sonorously spread its rich harmony over the vast light-filled hall.") The dialogues begin before the first appearance of the refrain (II, 93) and continue until the music and counterdance stop (II, 116).

In part six are included separate lyric poems in an album that Angela's friend, Adelaida, examines when Angela leaves the room to see if her mother has gone out. This is a brief anthology of lyric poems attributed to Don Luis, Don Juan's friend who commits suicide (II, 306–310). These poems have been praised for beauty and melody.[114]

It is desirable to look for social criticism, autobiographical reminiscence, patriotic sentiments to derive maximum enjoyment. These aspects attract modern readers,[115] though they were regarded as evidence of unpoetic fumbling by earlier readers.[116]

An example of realism is an episode in part four of the poem. Don Juan is taken to jail, on suspicion, by a night patrolman and spends the night in jail with three of his acquaintances who had been arrested after the fight in the theater that ensued after the public humiliation of Angela. Don Juan suggests that they purge their sin by drinking maté or Paraguay tea, when some mice make their presence known by squealing. The men succeed in catching one of the mice and killing it amid excited laughter (II, 247). This is lively, though not what readers of epic poems have been led to expect.

The Fallen Angel has much that is interesting in it, but the interest is scattered and may not exert a sustained appeal to the majority of readers. Its neglect is unfortunate.

For the admirer of Echeverría, the poem is rewarding. It concludes optimistically with the hope of an Argentina free of Rosas's despotism (II, 540–541). In this passage Rosas is a Minotaur hungrily roaring for blood.

The Fallen Angel must count as a valiant effort from a man whose circumstances at the time of composition excite compassion. As a piece of evidence is the following description of Echeverría at this time by a man who later became president of Argentina, Bartolomé Mitre:

En aquella época, Echeverría vivía en un cuarto aislado, triste y desnudo, que bastaba a sus gustos modestos y sencillos . . . Compraba por cuadernillos en la pulpería inmediata la cantidad de papel ordinario que había de consumir en el día y muchas veces el papel era tan malo que no se podía escribir en él . . . Sereno, afectuoso, con ilusiones de niño, con emociones de hombre y con las ideas del genio que une la inspiración a la meditación . . . nos leía algunas estrofas de su *Angel caído* recientemente escritas, en que se veía la musa jadeante que tendía con dificultad sus alas doloridas."[117]

("At that period, Echeverría lived in a lonely room, sad and barren, which was sufficient for his modest and simple needs. He used to buy in little exercise books the amount of plain paper that he would use in a day at the neighboring general store and often the paper was so bad that it could not be written on . . . Serene, affectionate, with a child's illusions and a man's emotions and with the ideas of the temper that joins together inspiration and meditation . . . he would read to us some recently written stanzas of his

Fallen Angel, in which could be seen the breathless muse extending its pained wings with difficulty.")

Menéndez y Pelayo doubtless sincerely felt that the poem represented the fall of a poet, but actually the work is a triumph over odds. It might well have been named *Don Juan*, but Echeverría's tendency to idealize women makes it natural to have as title *The Fallen Angel*, which refers to the chief woman (or girl when she loses her innocence) in the poem, appropriately named Angela or, in diminutive form, Angelita (II, 9, 40, 524).

CHAPTER 4

THE LYRICS

Two months before Echeverría left France, the French literary critic, Charles-Augustin Sainte-Beuve, published a volume of *Consolations*, which may have influenced Echeverría in his choice of title for *Los consuelos (The Consolations)*.

I. *First Collection of Lyrics*

This collection of lyrics was successful when it appeared in 1834 and marks a concrete step in achieving his purpose of following new paths and seeking inspiration about him.

"Layda," already discussed as a longer narrative poem, is one of the thirty-seven compositions in the book, which is introduced by an epigraph from Ausías March in Catalán and its translation into Spanish by Fray Luis de León, with Echeverría's appeal that it be read by readers sad at the time or who have been so.[1]

"Lara o la partida" ("Lara or the Departure") (III, 15–21) seems to be the beginning of a narrative, preceded by an epigraph from Byron.[2] It places Byron's Chief of Lara on board ship on the river Plate, ready to cross "the bounding main" and to leave "in youth his father-land."[3] It has not been considered successful (Juicios críticos, V, x). There are other poems of departure. One is "Adiós" ("Farewell") (III, 60–62) with an epigraph from Victor Hugo.[4] It reflects the sentiment of a man forced to say farewell to his beloved, and his hope of seeing her again if death does not prevent. "A María" ("To María") (III, 127–131) treats the same theme. It is preceded by an epigraph from Camoëns.[5] It has been compared unfavorably to a similar poem by Byron: "Stanzas to Augusta," because of its sentimentality and overelaboration.[6] "Adiós en el mar" ("Farewell on the Sea") (III, 99–100) also has an epigraph from Camoëns, whose voyage to the Far East in exile and direct knowledge of the sea must have struck a sympathetic note in Echeverría.[7] These poems reflect a love of nature and the sea in various moods.

Life abroad is the subject of a poem called "Estancias" ("Stanzas") (III, 22–25) with an epigraph from Chateaubriand; the person who stays at home leads an idyllic existence.[8] Certain lines have parallels with passages from Italians, Guarini and Metastasio (Juicios críticos, V, xxii-xxiii). In a poem entitled "El regreso" (The Return") (III, 103–108) with an epigraph from Byron[9] the poet combines joy at returning to Argentina with the reflection of disillusion with Europe, where tyranny has triumphed; Switzerland is a lone exception.

The patriotism implied in "The Return" is a dominant element in other poems like "Profecía del Plata" ("Prophecy of the [river] Plate") (III, 30–35). An Argentinian poet, Vicente López y Planes, provides the epigraph,[10] The poem recalls a peninsular type made famous by Fray Luis de León, in his "Profecía del Tajo" ("Prophecy of the Tagus").[11] Echeverría's river utters a prophecy directed against tyrants of colonial days predicting the Inca's rising from his tomb in the Andes; in the poem reference is also made to the sun of May when Argentina won its independence. Patriotism is the theme of "A la independencia argentina" ("To Argentinian Independence") (III, 78–82) with an epigraph from Argentina's Esteban Luca.[12] "En celebración de Mayo" ("In Celebration of May") (III, 123–127) draws its epigraph from yet another compatriot, Juan Cruz Varela.[13] The spiritual identification of creoles and mestizos with the Indian, perhaps in thought more than in actuality, is hinted at in these lines: ". . . el Indiano, / Sus cadenas rompiendo, / Se ostenta independiente y soberano." (III, 124) (". . . the Indian, breaking his chains, shows himself to be independent and sovereign.")

Religious feeling and knowledge of the Bible inform certain poems. One is "Ruego" ("Prayer") (III, 43–45) with a Latin epigraph from the Psalms.[14] Spain's Azorín suggested that Echeverría would have desired this poem to be inscribed on a stone placed in a rural church to be read by passersby and that this would please him in his abode in the Infinite.[15] "El impío" ("The Impious [Man]") (III, 84–86) likewise has an epigraph from the Psalms.[16] It deals with the impious atheist, struck down by God's wrath, who has vanished from the face of the earth. Nydia Lamarque finds it literarily weak but spiritually vigorous.[17] Prayerlike is "Deseo" ("Desire") (III, 40–41), likewise with an epigraph from the Psalms.[18] In it the poet begs for oblivion. The sincerity of this desire has been questioned (Juicios críticos, V, xxxi, civ-cv). Yearning to leave the planet for a region of eternal harmony is the theme of "Extasis" ("Ecstasy") (III, 41–42) which is prefaced by an epigraph from Revelation.[19]

Nature poems include "El pensamiento" ("The Pansy") (III, 13–15) with an epigraph from Francisco de Rioja.[20] Two stanzas of the poem have been praised as exemplifying the poet's two great virtues: fluency and melodiousness (Juicios críticos, V, x). "Luna naciente" ("Rising Moon") (III, 26–27) with an epigraph from *Faust*[21] is a harmonious voicing of the relationship between the beauty of the moon and the poet's hopes. "Crepúsculo" ("Twilight") (III, 62–64) with the subtitle "en el mar" ("on the sea") is introduced by an epigraph from Zárate.[22] It won praise from Azorín.[23] It has been called one of the most completely successful of Echeverría's lyrics.[24] It is the only poem by Echeverría found in a recently reprinted collection of Spanish poems with English translation.[25] The final stanza, quoted from page 381, may serve to illustrate the quiet dignity of the poem, preserved in English: "It is the hour in which my beautiful illusions / Take shape and augment: / They touch reality and then begin to fade, / And to sink in the twilight's gloom."

"Al clavel del aire" ("To the Carnation of the Air") (III, 109–114) is unusual for its vivacity, both of content and varied meter. The carnation is compared to the poet's beloved. The author of the brief epigraph is Henry Kirke White.[26] It has won critical praise. (Juicios críticos, V, xxxii) "La Noche" ("Night") (III, 120–122) with an epigraph from Moreto[27] finds Nature and the poet's frame of mind in accord.

Music seems to be the main theme of "La melodía" ("Melody") (III, 67–69) which has an epigraph from *The Tempest*.[28] Shakespeare seems to have been associated with music in Echeverría's mind. An interesting poem with an epigraph from Shakespeare's *Othello*, is "Imitación del inglés" ("Imitation of the English [poet]") (III, 76–77).[29] The poem is much closer textually to Desdemona's song or *romanza* in the last act of Rossini's *Otello* than to Desdemona's song by Shakespeare from which the epigraph was taken.[30] Several expressions of the Rossini aria have exact counterparts in Echeverría's poem, only two of which correspond to anything in Shakespeare's willow song. Parallels include:

Rossini	Echeverría
(a) a'pie d'un salice	al pie de un sauce
(Meaning: at the foot of a willow)	
(b) il mormorio mesceva	mezclaba su . . . rumor
(mingled its sound)	
(c) salce d'amor	sauce del amor
(willow of love)	
(d) l'ingrato	(a)l ingrato
([to] the ungrateful [one])	
(e) i ruscelletti limpidi	el manso arroyo
(Shakespeare's "the fresh streams")	
(f) mesti sospiri e pianto	lágrimas tristes
(Shakespeare's "salt tears")	

There is another poem with the same title, "Imitación del inglés" ("Imitation of the English [poet]") (III, 35–37) with an epigraph from Lope de Vega.[31] It is less clearly an imitation of Shakespeare than the one just discussed. Lope de Vega, of course, was Spain's equivalent in some ways to England's dramatist. The general situation is sorrow for the death of a young woman. The title may be in error for "Imitation of the Spanish [poet]." If this hypothesis can be sustained, an imitation of Lope may be the intention. Akin to this subject is that of "Recuerdo" ("Remembrance") (III, 29–30) with an epigraph from Thomas Campbell.[32] There is a note of hope that the image of the beloved will live in the poet's heart during his lifetime, and that his remains will be united with hers by death. The poem has been praised except for the final line, deemed "ugly": "y todo extinga" ("and extinguish everything") (III, 30) (Juicios críticos, V, xxxi).

"El poeta enfermo" ("The Sick Poet") (III, 37–40) is preceded by an epigraph from Jorge Manrique.[33] Here the theme of sorrow and death is intimated. Both Menéndez y Pelayo and Varela praise the poem highly[34] "Contestación" ("Answer") (III, 46–49) has an epigraph from the Cuban poet, Heredia.[35] The poet, in his sorrow, compares himself with a phoenix being consumed in fire. "Mi destino" ("My Destiny") (III, 64–67) has an epigraph from Victor Hugo.[36] This poem shows an obsession with death. Echeverría's chronic illness and constant feeling that death was near may add to the poignancy of the poem for readers familiar with the poet's life. Another poem of similar theme is "Mi estado" ("My State") (III, 82–84) introduced likewise by a Hugo epigraph[37] Posey compares this poem with Byron's "On This Day I Complete My Thirty-Sixth Year." The poems are similar in stanzaic form and length of lines and there is a kinship underlying the ideas. Posey feels that in the Argentinian self-pity and self-adulation replace the English poet's vigor and mercilessness with himself.[38] Lamarque finds this poem the expression of the poet's sick soul; if this is true, self-pity and self-adulation may be more appropriate.[39] "Estancias" ("Stanzas") (III, 101–103) with the epigraph attributed to George Crabbe reflects the same sort of hopelessness. Echeverría's epigraph reads "Without a hope in life" and is very similar in meaning to a line of Crabbe's "The World of Dreams" that reads "And I without a hope remain!"[40] "El infortunio" ("The Misfortune") with a subtitle "en el mar" ("on the sea") (III, 108–109) has an epigraph from Lamartine and has been praised by Azorín.[41] This poem is short, rapid, simple in expression. Many of the poems emphasize a change in attitude, from a hope-filled youth to a premature hopelessness. "Melancolía" ("Melancholy") (III, 119–120) is one of the shortest of the poems, and is introduced by an epigraph from Calderón.[42] It shows concern for the reaction of the beloved to the poet's tears and indifference to her. This poem, too, has won praise. (Juicios críticos, V, xxx) It is concise, clear, and restrained.

"El cementerio" ("The Cemetery") (III, 115–119) with two epigraphs, from Calderón and from Young[43], has been subjected to heavy attack (Juicios críticos, V, xxvi-xxvii, xxx). It has been called "one of the two worst poems" in the collection. Lamarque has called attention to the influence of Chateaubriand on this specimen of the graveyard school of Romantic poetry.[44] To the reader in quest of autobiographical elements in these poems the introduction in this poem of the voice of the poet's deceased mother from her grave is of interest. He hears an ineffable voice that he became familiar with from the cradle: ". . . ven, hijo mío, / Ven, te consolaré; ¡qué infeliz eres! / Tu alma no es de ese mundo, aquí es su centro: / El lodo es del reptil." (III, 118) (". . . come, my son, come, I shall console you, how unhappy you are! Your soul is not that of that world, here is its center, mud is the reptile's.") Here there is a contrast between *aquí*, "here," where the mother is and *ese mundo*, "that world" in which Echeverría is living, which is not the world of the soul. If the conventions of the graveyard school be accepted, the information gained from this interview with the poet's departed mother is both personal and also encouraging of hope in the immortality of the soul. The poem is made of a variety of elements, and is unique in *The Consolations*. An American reader may find that it stimulates the imagination somewhat as do some of Poe's tales of the macabre. In any case, Echeverría's "The Cemetery" must not be read as an exercise in logic.

Sorrow, resulting from meditation on history, is reflected in "La historia" ("History") (III, 50–60) with an epigraph from Byron.[45] This poem, dedicated to Juan María Gutiérrez, bears an early date, August of 1827, at Paris. It deals with the transient nature of earthly civilizations. Somewhat unusual in this collection of lyric poems is the recourse to notes by Echeverría to explain historical references to such figures as Cambyses, Philip of Macedon, or Manlius Capitolinus. It is a "fragment" and might have led to some mention of the New World's civilizations as well as those of the Old.

Another theme is that of love, sometimes entwined with other subjects like absence or death. "Los recuerdos" ("Remembrances") is a ballad dedicated to Delmira (III, 69–75) with an epigraph from Schiller.[46] Its theme is early love; there is some sorrow, but the poet hopes that the beloved's divine light may still shine on his sufferings. Love is dominant in a two-part poem in dialogue form with an epigraph from Schiller[47] with the title "El y ella" ("He and She") (III, 86–99). The opening of the second part was set to music as a song by Juan Pedro Esnaola dated June 29, 1835, after the publication of the volume.[48]

Finally must be mentioned two compositions with the same title: "Coros" ("Choruses") (III, 131–139) with an epigraph from Goethe[49] and (III, 140–142) one from Manzoni.[50] The first composition contains five individual choruses reminiscent of *Faust*; the second one includes two choruses which enjoin mortals and sinners to follow the guidance of the Christian God.

In a survey of some thirty separate poems it is hard to do much more than suggest themes, identify sources of epigraphs (always well chosen and revealing of Echeverría's literary experience and taste), and indicate some of the critical reaction to the poems. They have not usually been accorded detailed treatment as individual compositions, but there is enough variety to make hazardous generalizations that would be valid for them all. The use of the epigraph, the use of rhyme, avoidance of the sonnet form—these are generalizations that can be made, but they are of limited usefulness.

II. Serious Poems and Song Texts

In 1837 was published the collection *Rhymes*. Besides "The Captive Woman" it contains two serious poems of philosophical, religious nature, and seven poems destined for musical setting. The philosophical tendency is suggested by Moreto's motto-like phrase chosen as epigraph for the collection, which asks what poetry is if not philosophy.[51] The success of the volume is demonstrated by the fact that even during Echeverría's exile when Rosas was still in control of Buenos Aires, a second edition was published there. One of the song texts enjoyed as great a success as did "The Captive Woman."

The "Himno al dolor" ("Hymn to Pain") (III, 158–170) is prefaced by a Biblical epigraph, in Spanish rather than Latin, from Job, 5:6 and 6:7. In a note, Echeverría explains that he found the philosophical basis of his hymn in a comment by Kant on the Stoic who said that pain was never to be confessed as evil.[52] The poem has been called Echeverría's most beautiful lyric composition.[53] Bartolomé Mitre noted that it was an imitation of Lamartine's poem of similar title, "Hymne à la douleur." ("Hymn to Pain")[54] Lamarque has found it one of his best poems.[55] She points out how in the course of the poem the challenge to pain is transformed into a recognition of its purifying effect.

"Al corazón" ("To the Heart") (III, 171–175) likewise has an epigraph from Job, 6:8. It could be read as a sequel to the "Hymn to Pain" and ends with the poet's wish for eternal oblivion and for something that can calm the hell of his passions.

A group of seven poems goes under the heading "Canciones" ("Songs"), and has an epigraph from Camoëns[56] (III, 176). These are not all the song texts by Echeverría. Sometimes it is difficult to identify a text for a known song; Virgilio Rebaglio, founder of the Academy of Music in Buenos Aires under the protection of Bernardino Rivadavia, in pre-Rosas days, is the composer listed for Echeverría's "La noche, canción" ("Night, song") which may or may not be the same as his "The Night" (III, 120).[57] Some texts were set to music for guitar rather than piano; Esteban Massini and Manuel Fernández are mentioned in this connection.[58]

"La ausencia" ("Absence") (III, 176–177) is one of the songs set to music for pianoforte by Esnaola.[59] This text is pervaded with gentle melancholy.

"La diamela" ("The Jasmine") (III, 178–179) was also set to music by Esnaola.[60] Apparently the word refers to the Arabian jasmine. Lanuza has related, with some doubt, the text to the "Letters to a Friend," especially the thirtieth letter, dated February 8.[61] Here Echeverría speaks of meeting at a dance party at the home of a certain Donã Ana an amiable and beautiful woman named Luisa (V, 67). He speaks to her and dances with her. She made a deep impression: ". . . su dulce imagen me llena aún de delicia." (V, 71) (". . . her sweet image still fills me with delight.") Lanuza suggests that perhaps this Luisa had given to the poet the Arabian jasmine. Interestingly enough, between the time of the publication of *Rhymes* with certain words and that of the publication in *El cancionero argentino (The Argentinian Song-Book)* with Esnaola's music, there was a change in the wording. The former one is reproduced by Gutiérrez for the passage in question: "Desde entonces, do quiera que miro / Allí está la diamela olorosa, / Y a su lado una imagen hermosa / Cuya frente respira candor;" (III, 178) ("Since then, wherever I look there is the fragrant Arabian jasmine, and beside it a beautiful image whose brow breathes forth innocence.") Lanuza quotes the same lines as they appear in the *Song-book; olorosa*, "fragrant" has become *preciosa*, "beautiful," and there are other slight changes, but the last line is completely transformed to "de la bella que a mí me engañó"[62] ("of the fair one who deceived me.") Lamarque provides a different interpretation, also based on the life of the poet; it may not be incompatible with Lanuza's if the possibility of a change in name is recognized.[63] Lamarque points out that the poem had been written at least two years before its publication in

Rhymes. According to the tradition of the Gutiérrez family, Echeverría wrote it for the sister of Juan María Gutiérrez. Her name was María de los Angeles Gutiérrez. The act commemorated by the poem, the giving of a flower to the poet, most probably was done by the person for whom the text was composed. Lamarque pursues her commentary indicating that the gift of the flower would encourage the suitor, and that a proposal would be the next step. In that case, because of Echeverría's being father of an illegitimate daughter, María de los Angeles Gutiérrez must have rejected him. Lamarque supports her theory by reference to one of Echeverría's miscellaneous *Pensamientos* ("Thoughts") wherein he describes the angelic smile of a certain young woman who attracted his attention. He goes on: ". . . Sin embargo, yo no la amo aún; no la amo con todo el fuego de mi corazón, porque el orgullo me enfrena. Amar a una mujer que no siente como yo, que no está identificada con todo mi ser . . . imposible! . . ." (V, 448) ". . . Nevertheless, I do not love her yet, I do not love her with all the fire of my heart, because pride checks me. To love a woman who does not feel as I do, who is not identified with all my being . . . impossible! . . ." This statement seems psychologically significant, whether or not it explains the background of "The Jasmine."

The success of the song was complete and even in this century, as Lamarque remarks, all Argentinian women knew the words of the song by heart.[64] The words must be a factor in the song's popularity. The fact that the woman is unnamed in the song may have tempted speculation and added to its appeal. The last line is also ambiguous: "A ella sola consagro mi amor." (III, 179) ("To her [or it] alone I consecrate my love.") The word *ella* applies equally to the woman who bestowed the jasmine, and to the jasmine in Spanish; it is difficult to preserve this doubt in English.

If the songs are to be viewed as forming a cycle, there is an absence, followed by the gift of a flower, and next comes "A una lágrima" ("To a Tear") (III, 179–180) which suggests the relationship of a tear to love. The tear is compared with a pearl. This song was set to music by José Tomás Arízaga.[65]

Next in the presumed cycle is "El desamor" ("Indifference") (III, 180–182) set to music by Esnaola for piano and by Massini and Fernández for guitar.[66] This poem expresses distress and inability of the narrator to find consolation. An adjective in the song suggests that the text reflects a woman's feelings: "Pero una voz secreta / Me dice: infortunada! / Vivirás condenada / A eterno desamor" (III, 181). ("But a secret voice says to me: 'Unfortunate woman! You will live condemned to eternal indifference!' ") The ending of *infortunada* and of *condenada* is feminine singular, so that a woman's point of view seems to be mirrored.

In "La aroma" ("The Perfume") (III, 182–183) returns the motif of the flower. This was set to music for piano by Esnaola, and for guitar by Massini.[67] Here the beloved places a flower in her bosom.

"Serenata" ("Serenade") (III, 183–184), set to music by an anonymous composer[68], also included in part in the "Letters to a friend" between letters

64

dated February 17 and February 24, letters numbered 20 and 21. (V, 48) A note of Gutiérrez says that this text first was published in the first number of *El Recopilador* in 1836. The poem or song brings into play the guitar: "Angel tutelar que guardas / Su feliz sueño, decidla, / Las amorosas endechas / Que mi guitarra suspira." (III, 183–184) ("Guardian angel who keepest her sleep happy, relate to her the amorous dirges whispered by my guitar.")

The final song of this set is "La lágrima" ("The Tear") (III, 185–186). Lamarque explains that this text fits the theory that the cycle reflects a love suit on the part of the poet.[69] The woman, finally reduced to tears, discovers that the poet is himself incapable of tears, and of feeling love,—this is what she derives from the text of the poem. Then Lamarque enters into the realm of conjecture; perhaps the young woman repented and sought for reconciliation; the poet's pride prevented his responding to the change of heart. Love's perversity, in any case, seems to be in play.

There are two songs by Echeverría with piano score by Esnaola in Alberto Williams's modern collection of songs.[70] One is set to the song from the second part of "He and She" of *The Consolations* (III, 94) with only the first stanza's words printed.[71] The other is entitled "El ángel" ("The Angel") and begins "Llena de pena el alma" ("My soul full of pain").[72] From Williams's edition the words may be extended."[73]

Anonymous is the composer who set to music from *The Consolations* a poem called *Simpatía*, ("Sympathy") (III, 28).[74] Nor is a composer listed for the setting of the Canción ("Song") from *Elvira* (I, 10)[75] Esnaola was the composer of the music for another poem, "My Destiny," from *The Consolations*.[76]

Other poems from his hand set to music which are not from *The Consolations, Elvira,* or *Rhymes* are: "El desconsuelo" ("Disconsolation") (III, 347–348);[77] "A unos ojos" ("To a Pair of Eyes") (III, 361–362) also entitled "Los ojos negros" ("The Dark Eyes");[78] and "El deseo" ("Desire").[79] This makes up a total of sixteen poems that are part of the song repertory of Argentina, probably not a complete list.

The seriousness with which Echeverría regarded the song may be recognized by the pages he wrote concerning "Proyecto y prospecto de una colección de canciones nacionales" ("Project and Prospectus of a Collection of National Songs") and "La canción" ("The Song") (V, 130–137). He describes his plans to collaborate with Esnaola and to publish a series of songs called "Melodías argentinas" ("Argentinian Melodies") (V, 131). Echeverría mentions the need to avoid heroic song because of the political climate of Argentina under Rosas, but proposes that themes be sought in the soil, in the heart, and in social life. He reveals his esteem for Spain's ballad tradition, and his feeling that the introduction of Italianate verse by Boscán and Garcilaso de la Vega was unfortunate since that caused the older traditional verse to lose favor (V, 133–134). He also praises the ballad compositions of Béranger in France, Thomas Moore in Ireland, and Robert Burns in Scotland, as well as the similar efforts in Germany by Goethe and Schiller.

All in all, his interest in this type of literature fits into his design to enrich and develop Argentina's national literature.

III. Poems Rescued from Oblivion

Some other poems by Echeverría deserve listing from the body of works posthumously collected by Gutiérrez. There are, however, others that were intended only for the album of a friend or acquaintance, or that were incomplete, and not in finished form. At least one poem not by Echeverría was included, "Noches de diciembre" ("December Nights") by Bartolomé Mitre.[80] Two are translations, not recognized as such by Gutiérrez. These include "Comala," the name of the heroine of a dramatic poem (III, 258–268) which is translated from James Macpherson's pseudotranslations of the poems of Ossian,[81] and "Los tres arcángeles" ("The Three Archangels") (III, 302–304), translation of the prologue of Goethe's *Faust*.[82]

It seems desirable to concentrate here on poems which shed light on Echeverría's work as a whole, have a clear connection with his life, or have considerable individual merit.

"La barquerilla" ("The Little Boatgirl") (III, 208–213) is a *balata* or "dance song." This is an excellent example of the theme of the betrayed maiden, and in it Echeverría makes use of the altered refrain with good success.

Two selections (III, 220–221 and 221–224) are designated as fragments from a projected narrative poem, a "Pelerinaje de Gualpo" ("Pilgrimage of Gualpo"), which would have borne the relation to Echeverría that "Childe Harold's Pilgrimage" did to Byron. Echeverría made prose sketches for his poetry, at least on some occasions, and there is a prose selection for some of this material (V, 1–20). Comparison reveals that in the process of converting prose into verse, a real transformation took place.

One poem, "A D. J. M. F." ("To Don J. M. F.") (III, 242–243) is subtitled "dedicatoria de *Elvira*," ("dedicatory to *Elvira*"). It will be remembered that Dr. José María Fonseca, a friend of Echeverría whom he met on the occasion of his European trip, was the man to whom *Elvira* was dedicated. There is a letter dated at Paris 16 November, 1829 from the poet to the doctor in which he states his view that art should revolve in the circle of general ideas, encompassing all humanity, if possible. Cervantes, in *Don Quixote*, in the opinion of Echeverría, captured universal admiration by means of his personification of the ridiculous side of man. In the poem, Echeverría credits Fonseca with having inspired him in his efforts at composing poetry.

"A la pirámide" ("To the Pyramid") (III, 268–275)is the title of some fragments that refer to the change from the blue of independence to the black of tyranny and the bravery and patriotism symbolized by the pyramid. This honors the pyramid of May, between the home of Belgrano and the Citadel of Tucumán, which had been built after the battle of Tucumán, mentioned in the third section of the first canto of *Avellaneda*.

Another fragment is "Peregrinación de Don Juan" ("Pilgrimage of Don Juan") (III, 280–281). This is related by title to Byron's *Childe Harold* and *Don Juan* as well as for the character and theme to *The Fallen Angel*. Here is portrayed the amazement with which Don Juan viewed the monuments, theaters, palaces, portents of industry and art contained in Paris, a worthy successor of Athens and Rome.

Another selection is a discarded part of *Insurrection of the South*, felt as inappropriate at the time of the poem's publication (III, 289–296).

Another incomplete poem is "Al Dr. D. José María Fonseca" ("To Dr. Don José María Fonseca") in which the author seems to confide to Dr. Fonseca the story of his youth (III, 329–332). It is followed by the so-called "Último canto de Lara" ("Lara's Last Song"), suggestive of links with Byron and with Echeverría's "Lara or the Departure" in *The Consolations* containing toward its close lines very similar to those of the preceding fragment (III, 333–334). For example, in the former piece, Echeverría states: "Todo mira con ojo indiferente / Mi triste corazón y nada siente" (III, 330. ("My sad heart looks at everything with indifferent eye and feels nothing"). In "Lara's Last Song" the similar lines read: "Todo mira con ojo indiferente / Su triste corazón, y nada siente" (III, 343). ("His sad heart looks at everything with indifferent eye and feels nothing . . ."). It is clear that Echeverría would never have used verses so similar in two different poems. There are numerous other such parallels.

Another fragment is "A mi guitarra" ("To My Guitar") and, though dated 27 November 1831, may have a relationship to the poet's conception of *The Guitar*, if Gutiérrez's comment is correct.

Two poems are inspired from the subject of May 25 and Argentina's independence, one written in Colonia del Sacramento in 1841, and the other in Montevideo in 1844, prepared for the celebration there chaired by Dr. Andrés Lamas (III, 365–391 and 391–400). The first one is called "El 25 de Mayo" ("May 25") and the second "El 25 de Mayo de 1844 en Montevideo" ("May 25, 1844 in Montevideo"). In the latter poem Echeverría introduces more than once the notable topographical feature of Montevideo, the Cerro or Cerrito (III, 393, 395, 396, 397) or hill on which is located the oldest lighthouse in the country with an old fort and fine view. From Colonia in May of 1841 comes another patriotic poem, "A la juventud argentina en Mayo de 1841" ("To the Argentinian Youth in May of 1841") (III, 407–412). Another occasional poem of interest is the tribute to the deceased fellow poet, "A D. Juan Cruz Varela" ("To Don Juan Cruz Varela") (III, 475–487) with subtitle "muerto en la expatriación" ("dead in exile"). It carries the date April, 1839, and an indication that it was written at Echeverría's brother's country estancia at Los Talas. Varela had left Argentina in 1829 to take refuge in Montevideo since he was identified as friend and spokesman for the former liberal leader, Bernardino Rivadavia. Many of the lines could apply to Echeverría as well as to Varela, and are moving, such as the reference to begging, though a patriot, the bread from a foreigner, hard and bitter, to share with his children and wife (III, 477).

Of course, Echeverría had no wife, but he did have a daughter, Martina.

The fact that a poem is not mentioned in this brief survey does not mean that it is without interest; the range of subject shown in these poems rescued for posterity by Gutiérrez is impressive. Among omitted poems are some that may show the influence of Shakespeare (III, 313–315 or III, 402–406) or what a poetic drama by Echeverría might have been like (III, 419–447). Changes in taste between 1851 and the first publication of many of these poems two decades later may account for the neglect into which they have fallen. It is not just to treat unfinished works with overcritical eye. Gratitude must be expressed to the devotion of Echeverría's friend and editor, Juan María Gutiérrez, for making these poems available to readers.

CHAPTER 5

A SOCIALIST DOGMA

A statue of Esteban Echeverría, now located in Buenos Aires near the Plaza San Martín with its huge monument to Argentina's hero, General José de San Martín, within view, shows the esteem in which he was held a century after his birth. The statue was inaugurated in 1907; it had been commissioned to be done by the sculptor, Torcuato Tasso, on the occasion of Echeverría's centennial through the initiative of the youth of the Colegio Nacional of Buenos Aires.[1] Thirty years later a plaque was placed below it stating that it was an offering to the poet, sociologist, educator, and tribune in the Dogma of May from the association of ex-students of the Colegio Nacional, a testimony to continued esteem. There are several inscriptions from his work around the base of the statue. Not one is from a poem; they reflect his concern with the Dogma of May.

It is profitable to look at the four quotations since they may be presumed to emphasize inspiring aspects of his thought: 1. "Hacer obrar a un pueblo en contra de las condiciones particulares de su ser como pueblo libre es malgastar su actividad, es desviarlo del progreso, es encaminarlo al retroceso" (IV, 19–20). ("To cause a people to act counter to the particular conditions of their being as a free people is to waste their activity, is to lead them away from progress, is to put them on the road to reversion.")

2. "Vosotros, Argentinos, lucháis por la Democracia de Mayo, y vuestra causa, no sólo es legítima, sino también santa ante los ojos de Dios, y de los Pueblos libres del mundo" (IV, 86). ("You, Argentinians, fight for the Democracy of May, and your cause not only is legitimate but also holy in the eyes of God, and of the free peoples of the world.")

3. "Miserables de aquellos que vacilan cuando la tiranía se ceba en las entrañas de la patria" (IV, 113). ("Wretched are those who hesitate when tyranny preys on the fatherland's entrails.")

4. "Los esclavos o los hombres sometidos al poder absoluto, no tienen patria porque la patria no se vincula a la tierra natal sino en el libre ejercicio de los derechos ciudadanos" (IV, 115). ("Slaves or men submissive to absolute power have no fatherland because the fatherland is not linked to the land of one's birth but to the free exercise of the rights of a citizen.")

I. The Parts of the Dogma

The first two quotations, not exactly as they appear in the printed text, are found in the explanatory "Ojeada retrospectiva sobre el movimiento intelectual en al Plata desde el año 37" ("Retrospective Glance over the Intellectual Movement in the Plate [region] since 1837") which precedes the actual "Dogma socialista de la Asociación de Mayo" ("Socialist Dogma of the Association of May"). These two parts may be considered to comprise the complete *Dogma socialista (Socialist Dogma)* as published in Monte-video in 1846. Between these two sections is an interesting reply by Eche-verría to the views of Antonio Alcalá Galiano, a Spanish critic, as expressed in three numbers (234, 235, 236) of the *Comercio del Plata* to the effect that Spanish-American literature was in its infancy and that it should return to the Spanish fold so as to achieve a high degree of splendor. Echeverría felt that Spanish literature of the nineteenth century was not a source for inspiration, since so much of it was imitative or relatively stagnant as com-pared with its Golden Age.

The "Retrospective Glance" has a dedication to sublime martyrs of Ar-gentina; this is followed by the story of the creation of the *Socialist Dogma* and the Association of May. The first quotation is from part three of this part; it states the necessity for the people to be free in order to take the road to progress away from colonial tyranny and slavery.

The second quotation is from part nine of the "Retrospective Glance," in which Echeverría explains that the members of the Association are fighting for country, against Rosas, for liberty, fraternity, and equality in order to put the fatherland on the peaceful course of true progress, summed up by the phrase "Democracy of May."

The third quotation is the sixteenth of forty-two statements that precede the section of Symbolic Words in the "Socialist Dogma" proper and is a plea to fight against tyranny. The Symbolic Words like Association, Prog-ress, Fraternity, Liberty, Equality, God are the means by which the "So-cialist Dogma" proper is organized.

The fourth quotation is the twenty-sixth of the forty-two statements and goes beyond the fight against tyranny to the need for citizens to practice their rights.

These quotations illustrate the style (recalling at times the Bible) and con-cerns of the document which has been called a primer for the building of a country.[2] This phrase emphasizes the basic nature of the Dogma. The ideas were shared by the members of the Association of May, which included not only Echeverría, who occupied a key role, but also Juan Bautista Alberdi, Juan María Gutiérrez and others of that generation, sometimes called the Generation of 1837. They had gathered for intellectual discussions in the Literary Salon using space that Marcos Sastre, bookseller and thinker, pro-vided. Rosas's regime had limited places for such discussions. Thus came recognition of the need to form a Young Argentina or Association with a Credo, Code, or Dogma about which to center their efforts toward a social and liberal regeneration in the course of the independence leaders.

II. The Views of Palcos on the Dogma

Alberto Palcos is the man who prepared the critical edition of the *Socialist Dogma*. The prologue is a basic, scholarly source of information on the work, its genesis, its significance, and the elements forming it.[3] Here are presented some of his chief conclusions. The first five Symbolical Words consist of the definition of general principles of the era. The application to Argentina's special condition is a feature of the last ten Symbolical Words. Echeverría's work is a strong, brilliant synthesis of ideas of various thinkers.[4] Palcos finds four chief external influences: a liberal Christian philosophy of the type associated with Félicité de Lamennais and Claude-Henri, Comte de Saint-Simon being first.[5] Second is the influence of Giuseppe Mazzini with his moral fervor and advocacy of nationalism, unity, and a European federation; Echeverría's scope is more limited, a desire for the intellectual and ethical regeneration of his country.[6] Third is the influence of the Utopian socialism of Saint-Simon as displayed in the works of Pierre Leroux.[7] This is the socialism of the *Socialist Dogma*, a type of social democracy in which society would be able to and expected to control abuses of individualism.[8] There is some similarity, possibly accidental, between some ideas of the *Socialist Dogma* and those of Victor de Considérant, disciple of Charles Fourier. It is possible that the earlier form of the *Socialist Dogma* exerted an influence on the French thinker.[9]

Palcos lists seven basic virtues of the work. It put May (the spirit of independence) in the position of axis about which the nation would rotate. This meant the reestablishment of a sense of historic continuity for Argentina; it emphasized a line of development toward progress and democracy, as opposed to the counterrevolutionary line represented by Rosas which tended to preserve the traditions of colonial isolation.[10] The second virtue is the insistence that Argentinians study themselves without reference to foreign models.[11] Thirdly is the need for synthesis between the concepts of fatherland and humanity and those of the individual and society.[12] It is perhaps not farfetched to see an influence of this on the justicialism of Perón: ". . . two pairs of opposing forces were constantly struggling for supremacy in society: idealism and materialism, individualism and collectivism . . . Justicialism . . . sought a balance that was not static and centrist but dynamic and fluid."[13] In both cases there are four factors to be put in balance or synthesized, and the needs of the individual are in both schemes. In this connection, Palcos mentions the influence of Rousseau's *Social Contract*; he suggests that Echeverría here has reconciled an opposition between Rousseau and Saint-Simon.[14] Palcos, of course, does not refer to justicialism. For Echeverría, society or association has as aim the guaranteeing of individual rights; if it violates these rights, the pact is broken and the association dissolved (IV, 172). Palcos relates this aspect of the *Socialist Dogma* to article 29 of the Constitution of Argentina; here we see still living the idea that Rosas was a traitor. Article 29 merits quotation: "Congress may not confer on the National Executive, nor the provincial Legislatures on the provincial Governors extraordinary powers, nor the whole of the public authority, nor grant them acts of submission or supremacy whereby the lives, the honor, or the property of Argentinians will be at the mercy of governments or any person whatsoever. Acts of this nature shall be utterly void, and shall render those who formulate or consent to them or sign them liable to be called to account and to be punished as infamous traitors to their country."[15] Beyond the duty of society to guarantee individual rights is the necessity of rule in accordance with the dictates of reason. Reasonable people must dictate the law (IV, 174–175). Thus suffrage must be limited until the masses are able to exercise it reasonably (IV, 177).

The fourth virtue seen by Palcos is the advocacy of a politics of principles, not of persons.[16] Individual men are important only in being the architects in realizing social ideals and as they represent the expression of the country's highest virtue and intelligence (IV, 90). This is an attitude against the power and influence of the caudillo. It is possible that Echeverría would have enjoyed seeing himself in the role of social architect. In this connection, Palcos quotes from a letter written by Echeverría to Félix Frías in Paris on April 8, 1850: "Nunca se me ha ocurrido que entre nosotros podría ganarse nada escribiendo versos. Sólo la deplorable situación de nuestro país ha podido compelerme a malgastar en rimas estériles la substancia del cráneo[17] (V, 431). ("Never did it occur to me that among us anything could be gained writing verses. Only the deplorable situation of our country was able to compel me to waste the substance of my brain in sterile rhymes.") The word *ganar*, "to gain," may refer to economic gain, but also to achievement or success in the social or political field.

The fifth virtue for Palcos is the lesson of democracy, equated with May and progress in the *Socialist Dogma*.[18] Palcos quotes with high praise from the fourteenth Symbolic Word Echeverría's synthesis of Argentinian democracy toward which politics, philosophy, religion, art, science, and industry must all contribute (IV, 191–192). This passage for Palcos represents Echeverría at his best and earns for him eminence among the true sociologists and political thinkers of the nineteenth century.[19]

The sixth virtue lies in the recognition that the young generation must put aside the hate and discord existing between Federalists and Unitarians and work in harmonious reconciliation.[20]

The seventh virtue lies in the recognition that reason is not the monopoly of either Federalists or Unitarians; the Symbolic Word in which this idea is set forth is due to Echeverría's friend, Juan Bautista Alberdi. This is the fifteenth or last of the parts into which the "Socialist Dogma" is divided.[21] It was reproduced by Alberdi in his *Bases y puntos de partida para la organización política de la República Argentina (Bases and Points of Departure for the Political Organization of the Argentinian Republic)* in 1852. Links between the *Socialist Dogma* and Alberdi's work are evident, as they are between the *Bases and Points of Departure* and the Constitution of Argentina.

Echeverría sent a copy of the *Socialist Dogma* to the Governor of Entre Ríos, Justo José de Urquiza, and one to the Governor of Corrientes, Joaquín Madariaga, with accompanying letters dated September 19, 1846.[22] In 1852

Urquiza was to defeat Rosas and force the despot into exile. It is hard to measure the effect of the book and the letter on Rosas's fall, but they may have helped Urquiza to realize the need for change.[23]

An interesting document for the relevance of Echeverría to the modern political South American world is a commemorative speech delivered by Representative Luis Bernardo Pozzolo on April 25, 1973 at the Chamber of Representatives of the Oriental Republic of Uruguay. The occasion was the Day of the Americas, and the subject of the address was Esteban Echeverría's personality.

Pozzolo praises the spirit of Echeverría and his hope that there never will be extinguished in his homeland or in the Americas the proud sound of the trumpets of May, and points out sadly that: "Los principios de la democracia, y la misma democracia como figura y como forma de todas las justicias, aparecen aún como inmensa constelación oscurecida."[24] ("The principles of democracy and democracy itself as image and as form of all justices, appear still as an immense darkened constellation.") He points out that in Latin America many people still suffer exploitation and that more than half of the population of Latin America support "formas de gobierno donde la voluntad del pueblo ha sido reemplazada por la voluntad unipersonal de castas 'restauradoras.'"[25] ("forms of government wherein the will of the people has been replaced by the individual will of 'restoring' castes.") The use of the word "restauradoras" or "restoring" reminds a reader of the title given to the despot Rosas, "Restaurador de las Leyes," ("Restorer of the Laws.") Thus Pozzolo is characterizing the governments for over half Latin America as rule by despots, and in the context of his address, Echeverría's goals are not yet achieved. For Pozzolo Echeverría formulated the still desirable goal: "la creación definitiva de una América común, de una América finalmente hermanada por todas las formas de la civilización."[26] ("the definitive creation of a common America, of an America finally joined by all forms of civilization.") And the address he concludes with a quotation from the "Socialist Dogma," from the eleventh Symbolic Word, "emancipación del espíritu americano," ("emancipation of the American spirit"): "La política Americana tenderá a organizar la democracia, o en otros términos la igualdad y la libertad, asegurando, por medio de leyes adecuadas, a todos y cada uno de los miembros de la asociación, el más amplio y libre ejercicio de sus facultades naturales. Ella reconocerá el principio de la independencia y soberanía de cada pueblo, trazando con letras de oro en la empinada cresta de los Andes a la sombra de todos los estandartes americanos, este emblema divino;—*la nacionalidad es sagrada*. Ella fijará las reglas que deben regir sus relaciones entre sí, y con los demás pueblos del mundo" (IV, 167). ("American politics will tend to organize democracy, or in other terms equality and liberty, assuring, by means of adequate laws, to all and each one of the members of the association the broadest and freest exercise of their natural faculties. It will recognize the principle of the independence and sovereignty of each people, marking out on the lofty crest of the Andes in the shadow of all the American banners, this divine emblem;—*nationality is sacred*. It will fix the rules that must govern their interrelations, and their relations with the other peoples of the world.")

A recent dissertation has made use of the *Socialist Dogma*, especially Echeverría's reaction to the views of Alcalá Galiano, and some of his other writings to make a comparative study of the ideas of Echeverría, Gutiérrez, Alberdi, and Sarmiento with regard to Spain and the language of Spain.[27] Sara Jaroslavsky Lowy's conclusion is that the four thinkers felt a certain hostility toward Spain, that Spanish literature was lacking in originality, and that the goal should be a truly Spanish American national literature. The language of Argentina should not be under the control of the Royal Spanish Academy.[28] Echeverría's attitude is seen as less radical. The main basis for this assessment with regard to Echeverría is this section of the work; to this may be added one of the "Estudios literarios" ("Literary Studies") entitled "Estilo, lenguaje, ritmo, método expositivo" ("Style, Language, Rhythm, Expository Method") (V, 115–121). In this latter source, Echeverría praises Spanish for its ability to express spontaneous characteristics of the imagination and to depict material objects, and he says that, though he has not read any of them, the Spanish novels of chivalry of the Middle Ages are doubtless superior to those of other countries in brilliance and display of color (V, 117). He praises Spain for literary figures like Fray Luis de Granada, Lope de Vega, Fray Luis de León, Fernando de Herrera, Francisco de Rioja, Francisco de Quevedo, and Calderón de la Barca, but feels that since its Golden Age Spain has remained stationary and that it lacked writers of genius to regenerate its language and intellectual culture (V, 118). Art for art's sake might serve the needs of Germany, England, or France, but is not adapted to the needs of new societies or countries oppressed by tradition, colonial or otherwise (IV, 99). Echeverría challenges Alcalá Galiano by asking what modern Spanish names can compare with those of Benjamin Franklin, Thomas Jefferson, James Fenimore Cooper, and Washington Irving, respected in Europe as well as in America. He contrasts the democratic and civilizing tendency of North American society with the Spanish imperfect assimilation of French literature (IV, 104–107). Spanish literature of the Golden Age and the language itself are respected by Echeverría. He is not anti-Spanish. In fact, he states: ". . . la América . . . simpatiza profundamente con la España progresista, y desearía verla cuanto antes en estado de poder recibir de ella en el orden de las ideas, la influencia benefactora que ya recibe por el comercio y por el mutuo cambio de sus productos industriales" (IV, 107). (". . . [Spanish] America . . . deeply sympathizes with progressive Spain, and would wish to see it as soon as possible in the condition of being able to receive from it in the order of ideas, the beneficial influence that it now receives through commerce and through the mutual exchange of their industrial products.") Spain, in a sense, may hope to look to Spanish America for a model in regard to its ideological (and literary) regeneration and progress.

III. The Letters to Pedro de Angelis

Reaction to the *Socialist Dogma* as published in 1846 came from the editor of the *Archivo americano y espíritu de la prensa del mundo (American Archive and Spirit of the Press of the World)*, Pedro de Angelis, who was at the time in Rosas's favor, although he had first come to Buenos Aires at the invitation of the liberal leader, Bernardino Rivadavia, in 1826. In two "Cartas a Don Pedro de Angelis," ("Letters to Don Pedro de Angelis"), first published in Montevideo on July 18, 1847 (IV, 228–262 and 262–326). These extensive letters are closely related to the *Socialist Dogma* and expand them. Both in content and in expression they are full of interest.

Plays on words are frequent; Echeverría refers to the *American Archive* as the Prensa Mazorquera or Mazorca Press, contrasting with the "Press of the World" in the long name of the publication; the Mazorca was Rosas's secret organization. He speaks of the linguistic confusion of the editor, Neapolitan by birth, who published the *American Archive* in three languages, none of them well written, since the Restorer (of the Laws) or Rosas, like God, has inspired the headquarters of the editor of the publication with the confusion of tongues (IV, 257)! He speaks of the editor's reply to a letter written to him in Italian by a compatriot, done in Spanish, since the editor said he had forgotten his native language. In the period before the unification of Italy, it was perhaps natural for Pedro de Angelis not to be proficient in Italian. Echeverría describes him as "el napolitano degradado que osa apellidar *Condottieri* a Garibaldi y a Anzani; y *canalla vendida* a esos generosos italianos que han derramado su sangre en Montevideo por la causa de la libertad y del progreso, y conquistado la palma del heroísmo en los campos de San Antonio" (IV, 259). ("the degraded Neapolitan who dares call Garibaldi and Anzani mercenaries; and those generous Italians who have shed their blood in Montevideo for the cause of liberty and progress and won the palm of heroism on the fields of San Antonio scum who have sold themselves.") Garibaldi himself recorded that a certain M. Page, commander of the French brigantine Ducouadic, used the term *Condottieri*, "mercenaries," of the Italians.[29] The fields of San Antonio, the name of a small stream near Salto, a port on the Uruguay river, became famous on February 8, 1846 for the heroic performance of an outnumbered Italian legion and Uruguay marines and cavalry against Buenos Aires forces under General Servando Gómez.[30] Both Garibaldi and Anzani acquitted themselves admirably on this occasion.[31]

In the first letter, Echeverría devotes his attention to De Angelis, his shifts in allegiance from a liberal like Bernardino Rivadavia to a conservative like Juan Manuel de Rosas, from Unitarian to Federalist; Echeverría compares him to the Great Nazir of Thomas Moore's *Lalla Rookh*, Fadladeen, and quotes in a very faithful Spanish version a bit more than a paragraph of Moore's prose beginning[32] (IV, 232–233). Fadladeen was a real sycophant; in Moore's words, "His political conduct and opinions were founded upon that line of Sadi,—'Should the Prince at noon-day say, It is night, declare that you behold the moon and stars,' "[33] Echeverría pursues the comparison; Rosas becomes "Gran Sultaán" or "Great Sultan" to carry out the motif, and "la religión mazorquera" or "mazorca religión" corresponds to the Islam of Fadladeen (IV, 233). Not only is De Angelis compared to Fadladeen, Echeverría refers to his "carota amoratada" or "purple face" alluding to Shakespeare's Bardolph in the *First Part of Henry the Fourth*, of whom Falstaff said: "I never see thy face but I think upon hellfire and Dives that lived in purple . . ."[34] (IV, 237, 250–251), making fun of De Angelis's physical appearance. Echeverría adds to the allusions with some to Cervantes,—to Sancho Panza (IV, 237), to the *entremés* entitled *El retablo de las maravillas (The Altarpiece of the Marvels)* (IV, 255), and to Don Quixote's defiant quotation of Agrajes[35] (IV, 247).

Both letters are full of interesting details,—the first is directed personally at De Angelis, whereas the second explains and clarifies the content of the *Socialist Dogma*.

Perhaps the most valuable part of the second letter lies in the historical sketch and analysis of details of what Echeverría considers to be the organization of Argentina as an independent country. He stresses the need for democracy and progress (IV, 307). he equates localism with Federalism, centralism and unity with the Unitarians (IV, 272). Both are historically legitimate, but neither should dominate (IV, 277). Echeverría lists Unitarian goals and points out failings (IV, 290–293). It is their methods that Echeverría particularly criticizes (IV, 295–296). The need of municipal organizations had been insufficiently recognized (IV, 310). They are seen as the hope of civilizing the countryside (IV, 314–317). Echeverría's claim is to have set on the foundation of May rudiments of an Argentinian social doctrine, the first of his countrymen to make such an attempt (IV, 319).

CHAPTER 6

A SYMBOL OF ROSAS'S ARGENTINA
THE SLAUGHTERHOUSE

To Echeverría's friend, Juan María Gutiérrez, is due the preservation and publication of *El matadero (The Slaughterhouse)* in 1871. It first appeared in the *Revista del Río de la Plata*; in 1874 it was published again as part of the *Complete Works*.

Gutiérrez had the advantage of seeing the manuscript and of knowing the poet as well as having seen other works left in manuscript and never published, so that what he reveals in the preface he wrote for *The Slaughterhouse* has unusual interest. The fact that Echeverría himself did not prepare the work for publication means, however, that the complete truth of the work's genesis and purpose may never be ascertained beyond doubts.

I. *Gutiérrez's View of "The Slaughterhouse"*

These pages were not intended to be published in the form that Echeverría left them; they represent work done hastily and with naked realism, and thus permit a reader to glimpse the genius, even the soul of the writer. They are to be taken as stenographic scenes that later might be elaborated and serve as the basis for a "cuadro de costumbres" or "sketch of manners" (V, 210–211). Gutiérrez goes on to relate the work to Echeverría's desire to educate the masses for democracy and to suggest that the sketch identifies the origin of the *mazorca*, the name given to Rosas's secret society. The slaughterhouse was their rehearsal ground, their cradle, and their school (V, 212). The handwriting reveals emotion on the part of Echeverría, perhaps anger rather than fear, an anger that is displayed in irony. Gutiérrez says that had this manuscript fallen into the hands of Rosas, Echeverría would have "disappeared" at once. (V, 213). The colors of the sketch are bold and red, but not exaggerated since they are suitable to the theme. The presence of the young victim of the executioners of the slaughterhouse does not dull the colors, since he is characterized by the energy, moral integrity, and physical courage inspired in a man with heart by the feeling of offended honor (V, 213). Gutiérrez goes on to say that the scene of the "savage Unitarian" in the power of the Judge of the Slaughterhouse" and his henchmen is no invention but a reality repeated more than once in that period. The fictional element would be the language and bearing of the victim, the moral drawn, a projection of what Echeverría would have done if placed in a like situation (V, 213). Gutiérrez apologizes for preserving certain crudities of expression that characterize the participants in the tragic event. They are not of a sort to be imitated. Their use in context would exile them permanently from decent use (V, 213–214). Gutiérrez feels that *The Slaughterhouse* documents a true epoch of terrorism, and that it is a "página histórica, un cuadro de costumbres y una protesta que nos honra" (V, 214) ("historic page, a sketch of manners, and a protest that honors us"). According to Gutiérrez, Echeverría felt that the truth must be told.

II. Morínigo's View of "The Slaughterhouse"

Building on foundations laid by Gutiérrez and familiar with subsequent studies of this "historic page," Mariano Morínigo has provided a splendid assessment of the all-important elements in The Slaughterhouse: reality and fiction.[1] He points out that it resists classification, despite its having been called the first cuento, "tale or short story," in Argentina's literature. As he says, "no huele a cuento,"[2] ("it does not smell like a short story.") Or, "no nos parece un cuento, aunque narración breve y aunque no haya otro modo de designarlo."[3] ("it does not seem to us to be a short story, although a short narrative and although there may be no other way to designate it.") Quarrels over the genre it represents may be unimportant but force the critic to characterize it, to focus attention on elements in it: brevity, realism, and to think about the degree to which it may represent a finished, elaborated literary work.[4]

Moríngo emphasizes that Echeverría strove in the work to write Argentinian history.[5] But as an accusation against the viciousness of Rosas's regime, it is—for Morínigo—too subjective to be pure history.[6] In summary he says: ". . . el verdadero mérito de Echeverría . . . se proyecta más allá del área rioplatense, pues El Matadero no sólo es el primer cuento argentino, sino sobre todo el primero en descubrir para la literature hispanoamericana esta concepción originalísima de configuración literaria de la realidad-nación, que, al cabo de un siglo y más de vida independiente, se identifica con una de las formas más genuinas de vida y expresión hispanoamericanas. Pero esto Echeverría no lo supo."[7] (". . . the true merit of Echeverría . . . goes beyond the region of the River Plate, for The Slaughterhouse not only is the first Argentinian short story, but above all the first one to disclose for Hispanoamerican literature this extremely original conception of the literary configuration of the reality-nation, which, at the end of a century and more of independent life, is identified as one of the most genuine Hispanoamerican forms of life and expression. But this Echeverría did not find out.") The compound noun reality-nation is somewhat hard to explain; in The Slaughterhouse, as in some other Latin American works (like El Senõr Presidente (Mr. President) of Miguel Angel Asturias, Nobel-prize winner from Guatemala), the reality of the creation, a creation in which the narrator or author takes his stand as citizen of his country, can be identified as that country, the political regime of which is being condemned. Such works are propagandistic but characterize the author's country as well.

III. History and "The Slaughterhouse"

Morínigo, more than most critics, stresses the importance of history in regard to this work. Parts of the narrative do, indeed, seem like history, the type of history nowadays forming the content of "oral history," wherein a participant in a society reminisces, providing material and answers for later historians. What was it like to be living in Buenos Aires in 1839 under the regime of Juan Manuel de Rosas? Ideally, not only Echeverría would be asked this question, but others of the day; the details they would give would be of a sort not recorded in most formal works of history. They would supplement, and give a personal dimension. To view the work in this spirit does not falsify the purpose of drawing a parallel between the slaughterhouse of Buenos Aires and Argentina under the rule of Rosas. The use of the term "slaughterhouse" is not unique to this work in its application to Rosas's regime; it is thus used in *Insurrection of the South* (I, 269).

The first sentence of *The Slaughterhouse* is arresting: "Apesar de que la mía es historia, no la empezaré por el arca de Noé y la genealogía de sus ascendientes como acostumbraban hacerlo los antiguos historiadores españoles de América, que deben ser nuestros prototipos" (V, 209). ("In spite of the fact that mine is (a) history, I shall not begin it with Noah's ark and the genealogy of his ancestors as the old Spanish historians of America who must be our prototypes used to do.") This is an unusual beginning; if, however, the *Compendio y descripción de las Indias Occidentales (Compendium and Description of the West Indies)* is at all typical, Noah, the ark, and genealogy do find a place at the beginning, right after the geographical setting. The first sentence of the third chapter begins: "Después de la creación del mundo, pasados 1.056 años, nació Noé hijo de Lamec . . ."[8] ("After the creation of the world, 1,056 years having passed, Noah son of Lamech was born . . .") Echeverría does not give his reasons for beginning somewhat later, in the decade of the 1830's. He does not indicate the fourth of the numbers, thus leaving the exact year uncertain. A possible reason is that to go back to Noah would not be in the spirit of Americanizing the setting. Another reason might be that for him Argentina's history begins with May, in 1810, with independence. Echeverría could hardly be expected to follow the old Spanish New World historians in his own "history." Part of *The Slaughterhouse* corresponds to known history; some other details are so specific that, if it is admitted that Echeverría hoped that some day it might be read by people who had been living in that period, fiction seems unlikely. One statement demonstrably untrue would cast doubt on others; realism, truth, verisimilitude must be admitted as part of the work's inherent character.

Particularly is this true in the earlier part which gives the background to certain events taking place prior to the day of the main events of the narrative. This day is pinpointed as "el décimo sexto día de la carestia, víspera del día de Dolores." ("the sixteenth day of the shortage, day before the (feast of the Seven) Sorrows (of the Blessed Virgin Mary)." This identifies the day as Thursday in Passion Week, preceding Palm Sunday, since the feast day of the Seven Sorrows, in Echeverría's time, was on the Friday of Passion Week.

Briefly, before this day, during Lent a period of rains had set in, causing flooding and other inconveniences, so much so that some people thought that the Day of Judgment was about to arrive (V, 214–215). The Unitarians became the scapegoat; God was punishing their sins! Church bells were rung in petition to God by order of the "very Catholic" Restorer, Rosas, and a procession of the people, barefoot and bareheaded, headed by the Bishop holding the Host, to the Balcarce ravine, was planned in order to exorcise the Unitarian devil of the flood and implore God's mercy. This proved to be unnecessary since the waters receded and the crisis passed. Because of the flood for two weeks the slaughterhouse of the Convalescencia had no cattle to slaughter, and within two days the beef supply was consumed; the price of chicken, eggs, and fish soared. Doctors pointed out deleterious effects of the scarcity, whereas priests cried out against meat eating in Lent; stomachs were set at war with consciences, and the dietary change caused indigestion. The government arranged for more meat at the slaughterhouse; the day in question fifty fat steers were brought there, the first of which was made as a gift to Rosas (V, 217–220).

The year, not made definite by Echeverría in the text, can be determined by reference to the mourning for the late Doña Encarnación, wife of the Restorer. She died October 19, 1838, and just one Lenten period followed before 1840, excluded by Echeverría's indication of the decade.[9] Easter fell on March 31, 1839; Thursday before Palm Sunday was ten days before. The shortage began about March 5.

There is another historical reference, to the uprising to unseat Juan Ramón Balcarce, instigated by Doña Encarnación when Rosas was away. Balcarce had succeeded the first Rosas rule in 1832. October 11, 1833 was the date and General Agustín de Pinedo the military leader. Echeverría speaks of an anniversary of that revolution when the butchers made Doña Encarnación patroness of the slaughterhouse, at a banquet attended by leading Federalist ladies, after which her name was plastered on the walls of the *casilla*, "hut, shed," of that institution. The anniversary must have been no earlier than Rosas's return to power in 1835, so that the banquet would have been in October between 1835 and 1838.

Echeverría was still in Argentina during these years, so that he might well have heard eyewitness accounts, even if he had not been present. What is even more important in judging the probable historicity of "The Slaughterhouse," is that a fair proportion of the work's potential readers could compare his account with what they knew to have been true. The arrangement and choice of materials are of the artist, fusion of events not all taking place on a specific day may be admitted, but it is difficult to discredit Gutiérrez's view that "The Slaughterhouse" corresponds to fact, not to fiction.

Thus the narrative remains a document with historical validity. Echeverría wrote it as his *historia*, and whether this word be thought of as "history" or as "story," the possessive "his" shows that it is not likely that objectivity has been achieved. The work is an attack on the brutalization of the people, particularly those of the slaughterhouse, which took place under the despot. Some critics read it without sympathy for the denizens of the slaughterhouse but if viewed in the context of the *Socialist Dogma*, the account may reinforce the idea that the masses—rather than deserving the contempt of the reader—are not yet ready for suffrage, that they need to be civilized and educated, that there is hope for them after the removal of Rosas from power.[10]

The moralizing conclusion may be misleading. It is worthy of examination. After describing certain barbaric activities that took place there on March 21, 1839, the author concludes: "En aquel tiempo los carniceros degolladores del Matadero eran los apóstoles que propagaban a verga y puñal la federación rosina, y no es difícil imaginarse qué federación saldría de sus cabezas y cuchillas. Llamaban ellos salvaje unitario, conforme a la jerga inventada por el Restaurador, patrón de la cofradía, a todo el que no era degollador, carnicero, ni salvage, ni ladrón; a todo hombre decente y de corazón bien puesto, a todo patriota ilustrado amigo de las luces y de la libertad; y por el suceso anterior puede verse a las claras que el foco de la federación estaba en el Matadero" (V, 241–242). ("In that period the butcher executioners of the Slaughterhouse were the apostles who propagated with switch and dagger the Rosine federation, and it is not hard to imagine what sort of federation would come forth from their heads and cleavers. They called everyone not an executioner, butcher, savage, or thief, every decent man with heart well placed, every educated patriot fond of learning and of freedom, savage Unitarian, in accordance with the jargon invented by the Restorer [of Laws]; and through the aforementioned event it can clearly be seen that the focus of the federation was in the Slaughterhouse.") The intolerance of the regime is clear; the application of the term "savage Unitarian" to all those not one of them and the butchery of the *mazorca* are facts emphasized in Echeverría's close. Coming so closely upon the incident of the death of a young Unitarian in the hands of literal as well as figurative butchers, the statement has been interpreted as an exaltation of the Unitarian, rather than as an attack on the savagery of the Federalists of the day. It is hard to deny that Echeverría's sympathies are with the unfortunate victim, but the symbolism is directed more at the identity between the regime and the slaughterhouse with bloodthirsty butchers as henchmen.

The Unitarian who suffers at the butchers' hands is, in one possible view, merely one of the unfortunate sufferers, not an incarnation of every possible virtue.

IV. Easter and "The Slaughterhouse"

The fact that the events related in the narrative take place just before Easter has led David William Foster to interpret it in accordance with Paschal symbolism.[11] Foster has the events taking place on Good Friday, a basic flaw in his argument, since the *víspera de Dolores* clearly refers to a Thursday one week previous to Good Friday.[12] Foster's reading of the narrative with regard to the contempt Echeverría held the Church in for support of Rosas, and for a situation in which Rosas became almost a divinity of the Federalists can only be praised, since it highlights the irony of Echeverría.[13] And the idea that he presents, supported by apt quotation, that the Unitarian is in some way similar to Christ judged, tormented, and crucified is convincing, but more weight attaches to his dictum that "The Slaughterhouse" is an "elaboration of a primordial vision of a society within the framework of Christian symbology turned inside out.[14] Rosas was not God, the butchers were not Christ's disciples, and the Unitarian was not Christlike. This last verdict, that the Unitarian was not Christlike, finds support in his complete lack of patience and resignation. He brings on his own death in a tremendous display of will, and when offered water, he challenges the judge: "Uno de hiel te haría yo beber, infame" (V, 238). ("One of gall I would make you drink, villain.") In the Bible, Christ is offered wine, mingled with gall, but after tasting it, He does not drink.[15] The most cogent parallel between the Unitarian and Christ is in the following passage: "Mueran! Vivan! repitieron en coro los espectadores y atándolo codo con codo, entre moquetes y tirones, entre vociferaciones e injurias, arrastraron al joven al banco de tormento como los sayones al Cristo" (V, 236). ("May they die! May they live! repeated in chorus the spectators and tying him elbow to elbow, amid punches on the nose and sudden jerks, amid vociferations and insults, they dragged the young man to the seat of torture as the executioners (did) Christ.") The first two cries are intended to express the crowd's opposing attitudes: "May the Unitarians die!" and "May Rosas and Matasiete and the Federalists live!" The Unitarian is, thus, in a Christlike situation. Gutiérrez has suggested that the Unitarian is representative of Echeverría's ideal, how he would behave if placed in a similar situation. In details, however, the Unitarian is no duplicate. At the time of the events, Echeverría would be thirty-three years old, whereas the Unitarian was about twenty-five (V, 234). Matasiete is like Rosas and is a ringleader of the butchers; his name is symbolic, but may have been an actual nickname, since its meaning is "bully, braggart," and the elements *mata*, "(he) kills," and *siete*, "seven," are reminiscent of the tale of the little tailor who killed seven with one blow. The Judge is similar to Pilate; he prevents the beheading of the Unitarian before the mock trial (V, 236) and when the Unitarian dies, seems to try to evade responsibility: "Pobre diablo: queríamos únicamente divertirnos con él y tomó la cosa demasiado a lo serio" (V, 241). ("Poor devil: we merely wanted to have fun with him and he took the matter too seriously.")

V. Narrative in "The Slaughterhouse"

Historical background and religious symbolism are, of course, only relatively minor factors in the effect on a reader of "The Slaughterhouse."

The narrative proper begins after the reference to the fate of the first steer, presented to Rosas. The forty-nine remaining steers were killed within fifteen minutes, some with hides removed and others ready for skinning. Echeverría then gives a detailed description of the particular slaughterhouse where the events took place, not far from his home as a child. The cabin or hut is also described together with the allusion to Doña Encarnación. Different groups of people are described, and also mastiffs and seagulls overhead. In one part of the area some four hundred black women were kneeling to gather scraps and leavings. Some boys were throwing bladders or balls of meat at each other. Foul language could be heard despite the Restorer's prohibition and the holiness of the day. Other boys were engaged in a duel with knives. Echeverría, after a memorable description, states: "En fin, la escena que se representaba en el matadero era para vista no para escrita" (V, 227). ("In short the scene acted out in the slaughterhouse was to be seen, not to be written down.")

Against this background occurs the first individualized incident, the protracted killing of an animal that had characteristics both of bull and of steer. Coarse discussion follows dealing with the evidence provided by the animal's genitalia. In the excitement, a rope breaks loose from its pole, shooting through the air with the result that a child is decapitated to the amazement of those who had seen what had taken place. Meanwhile, the animal made its escape and was pursued by a number of men on horseback (V, 227–230). Much confusion follows, and as the bull heads toward the city, an Englishman on horseback approaches. His horse takes fright and throws its rider, who sinks into the mud. Once again the bull has caused an accident, this one less catastrophic but still dramatic and unplanned. The horsemen laugh at the poor Englishman; this is in accord with the xenophobia said to have marked the Rosas regime. Four black women collecting entrails and scraps are forced into a water-filled ditch to take refuge from the fleeing animal. The animal is cornered and brought back for Matasiete to kill him; at last it is ascertained that the animal in fact was a bull.

Bulls were forbidden in the slaughterhouse; the meat ought to have been thrown to the dogs, but in view of the meat shortage, the Judge thought it best to look the other way. Matasiete took for himself the brisket of *matambre* and, since it was noon and his work was done, he was on the point of leaving. Suddenly something else unexpectedly happens (V, 230–233). The incident of the young Unitarian, the part of the narrative that has caused "The Slaughterhouse" to be considered as a prime example of the Hispanoamerican short story, follows (V, 234–242). The crowd urges Matasiete to kill him just as he killed the bull, but the Judge intervenes and the young man is taken to the hut or cabin for a mock trial. Much of the scene is narrated through admirably vigorous exchange of dialogue. Events lead up to the preparation of the young man to be stripped and beaten; through what seems like a superhuman effort "un torrente de sangre brotó borbolloneando de la boca y las narices del joven y extendiéndose empezó a caer a chorros por entrambos lados de la mesa" (V, 241). ("a torrent of blood gushed seething from the young man's mouth and nostrils, and spreading, it began to fall in spurts on both sides of the table.") The deaths of the child and of the Unitarian, the presence of the bull in the slaughterhouse, the humiliation of the Englishman and of the black scavengers,—none of these were planned, but all of these came to pass, and the unusual is made to impress on the reader's mind the unusual savagery under the Rosas regime with the *mazorca*, after a few hours in the slaughterhouse with Echeverría serving as guide.

Whatever the genre, "The Slaughterhouse" is prose with a purpose, written with sincere emotion by an artist, but the emotion is under control. How much of the artistry is calculated is difficult to determine; the more the history, the less the imagination. But history, also, is an art. Honesty of reporting is not incompatible with calculation of effect. Morínigo denies that "The Slaughterhouse" is a carelessly executed sketch penned under the influence of anger, and states that Echeverría completed in it a final product, carefully elaborated. To take a possible illustration of planning, there are parallels in expression that emphasize a proportion between the death of the bull and that of the Unitarian, as shown by Pier Luigi Crovetto.[16] In the case of the bull, "brotó un torrente de la herida" (V, 232); in the case of the Unitarian, "un torrente de sangre brotó borbolloneando de la boca y las narices . . ." (V, 241), in translation "a torrent gushed from the wound" and " a torrent of blood gushed seething from the mouth and nostrils . . ." In another work, however, subject to needs of rhyme and meter, a similar occasion evokes expression not far removed in choice of words: "La yegua al lazo sujeta, / y a la boca de la herida / por donde ronca y resuella, / Y a borbollones arroja / La caliente sangre fuera, . . ." (I, 48) ("The mare tied by the lasso, and to the mouth of the wound, through which it roars and wheezes, and ejects seethingly the hot blood . . ." This incomplete passage comes from "The Captive Woman." It also provides a parallel between Brian and the Unitarian, both compared with a bull: "Echando espuma y herido / Como toro enfurecido / Se encaró; . . ." (I, 52) ("Emitting foam and wounded like an infuriated bull he confronted . . .") of Brian, and "Está furioso como toro montaraz" (V, 237) ("He is as furious as a wild bull") of the Unitarian. It is hard to decide which of these verbal likenesses correspond to planned and calculated emphasis within "The Slaughterhouse" and which are due to Echeverría's style and to parallel situations. For this reason, Crovetto's discussion remains suggestive rather than completely convincing. On one level, certain types of comparison may be favored by Echeverría. On another level, expression of this sort may be natural for any writer of that era and location with this type of subject. These comparisons had meaning for Echeverría, but how much significance do they have in an analysis of a single work as a unit? Certainly "The Slaughterhouse" succeeds in giving an illusion of spontaneity; some of its art may be the result of years of writing and long meditation on the brutality of Rosas's regime. A writer, too, may tailor his product to his perception of the expectations of his readers.

Crovetto's study impresses by its throughness, but its conclusions may not convince all readers: "È, ancora, in tutta questa serie di discorsi valutativi, nella loro specifica tramatura, nella loro valenza paradigmatica che si può scoprire l'entità e il segno di quella frattura insanabile consumata all'interno della società argentina del tempo di Echeverría . . . Ed è a tale frattura che ci si dovrà riferire per ricodificare soddisfacentemente il messaggio, la tesi del M(atadero); messaggio leggibile soltanto se calato nell'ottica manichea, esclusivistica e ferocemente anti-popolare che fu del teorico del liberalismo argentino."[17] ("It is, yet, in all this series of evaluative speeches, in their specific construction, in the paradigmatic valence that one may discover the importance and the measure of that irremediable fracture accomplished within the Argentinian society of Echeverría's time . . . And it is to such a fracture that one must refer in order to recodify in a satisfactory manner the message, the thesis of "The Slaughterhouse," a message readable only if placed in the Manichaean, exclusivistic, and ferociously anti-popular view possessed by the theoretician of Argentinian liberalism.") The fracture may be admitted, but to characterize Echeverría's view or "optics" as Manichaean (presumably dualistic), exclusivistic, and ferociously anti-popular is to state what is dubious, and what may be extremely misleading.

Is it anti-popular to blame bad conduct on the part of the masses on a tyrannical regime? The representations of evil in "The Slaughterhouse" are Rosas, Doña Encarnación, Matasiete, the butchers, the clergy, not the black women who are seeking scraps of meat, the mastiffs, the seagulls, the rats, the child decapitated accidentally, the Englishman forced into the mud in an undignified manner. Neither are the latter depicted as representations of good. A reader who fails to make careful comparisons may think that the Unitarian is the embodiment of good, a Christlike figure. As soon as the analogy relating the Unitarian to the sacrificed bull is carried to the Biblical parallel, the structure topples. Echeverría does not single out the exploited masses to display his sarcasm. He makes it clear that he feels that they have been brutalized under Rosas, the bosses, and the *mazorca*. If the appeal at the conclusion of "The Slaughterhouse" is allowed to speak for itself, it is clear that education and freedom can permit the masses to display their potential for good. The Unitarian does not stand for good,—he represents courage and is a victim of evil; eventually he tries to defy his taunters and is the direct agent of his death, though the bullies (not the masses, not the people) provide the incentive.

If the masses did not have Echeverría's respect, why the effort to demonstrate so constantly the brutalizing effect of despotism and lack of education on disadvantaged members of Argentina's society? The fact that some (or many) of them may have, in a material way, received benefits from Rosa's regime does not mean that they were not being exploited by him. As an individual, it is natural that Echeverría should have limitations in feeling sympathy for all sectors of society. His particular "blind spot" is not being able to admire the virtues of tyrants and bullies. In other works, like the *Socialist Dogma*, Echeverría gives indications of respecting aspects of

Federalism or localism and of recognizing failings of the Unitarians. His idealism led him to assume that with reason dominant, freedom of thought and of expression, the rights of the individual protected by an improved society, and newly regenerated people, neither Unitarians nor Federalists, a bright future existed for Argentina. Since he suffered from the climate of Rosas's rule, he doubtless exaggerated, but this is a different matter from reducing the message of *The Slaughterhouse* to an anti-popular, exclusivistic, dualistic presentation, even at a subconscious level.

It might even be suggested that Echeverría, by making the specially horrifying and depressing incidents the result of chance or of accident, reduces the sting of his attack. If the Unitarian had arrived after the departure of Matasiete, if the bull had not—against rules and against the usual state of affairs—been brought into the slaughterhouse, if the flood and scarcity of meat had not made the slaughterhouse the scene of unusually frenzied activity, the description of events there would probably have been tamer, "to be seen as well as to be written down," to vary Echeverría's words slightly. The lesson may be drawn: if people were free and educated, the horrors of March 21, 1839 would not have been possible even in the slaughterhouse. In an ideal society, such as that envisaged by Echeverría, the Church, or rather, the clergy, would not aid and abet tyrants. Though not involved directly in the events of the main narrative, in the introductory pages the clergy bear the brunt of Echeverría's displeasure. Anti-dictator, anti-*mazorca* might be identified by such labels,—not by the adjective "anti-popular" in the meaning of "against the people."

The Slaughterhouse is a work which continues to excite the imagination of its readers; it may be that Crovetto will provide the key for appreciation to some readers better than Morínigo or Gutiérrez. Other approaches, likewise, which reflect a sensitive and careful reading may be helpful. One such is that of Maria de José Queiroz.[18] Certain passages fill, in Queiroz's view, the function of the chorus in Greek tragedy. One instance of the "chorus" is in the introduction of the Unitarian, protagonist of the climactic and concluding act of the tragedy. Like Crovetto, Queiroz emphasizes parallels between the bull's death and the Unitarian's, the fact that they perform similar functions.[19] But she also emphasizes the capital difference: Matasiete kills the bull, but not the Unitarian, who dies through the exercise of his will power.[20] Her approach is literary and emphasizes the drama of "The Slaughterhouse." For her, with this work ". . . empieza el drama moderno en que se funden armónicamente la dignidad de la tragedia clásica y el vulgar y animado espectáculo del pequeño proletariado."[21] (". . . begins modern drama in which are fused harmoniously the dignity of the classic tragedy and the vulgar and animated spectacle of the petty proletariat.")

C. Enrique Pupo-Walker stresses a different fusion in his modern study of "The Slaughterhouse," that of short story within a sketch of manners. He also separates the conclusion from the short story proper which ends with the Unitarian's death,—the moralizing conclusion in which Echeverría clarifies the symbolism of the slaughterhouse. He describes it as a coda of journalistic prose.[22] If this is true, there is an obvious link between "The Slaughterhouse" and *Insurrection of the South*, where, in its first form at least, Echeverría acts almost as journalist or war correspondent, though in verse. Possibly the term coda is meant to deny a high level of artistic merit. Pupo-Walker has a high regard for the work, and concentrates on its place in the history of the Hispanoamerican narrative: "*El matadero no fue más que una prematura crisálida de cuento artístico que accidentalmente engendró la literatura costumbrista.*"[23] ("*The Slaughterhouse* was only a premature chrysalis of an artistic short story that the literature of sketches of manners engendered accidentally.")

"The Slaughterhouse" and the Sketch of Manners

A modern study by Juan Carlos Ghiano deals with Echeverría's masterpiece and its affiliation with peninsular Spanish sketches and manners, particularly those of Mariano José de Larra, as well as with two other works by Echeverría.[24] Knowledge of Larra's work cannot be questioned; Echeverría quotes from him by name[25] (V, 381).

The two works by Echeverría that serve as basis of comparison and may fit better the norms of Larra's works are related to each other in title. One was first published in the Buenos Aires *El Recopilador*, 7 May 1836 and is entitled "Apología del matambre" (V, 200–208). ("Apology of the Brisket").

It may be taken as a sketch of manners in the tradition of Larra, with the purpose of educating a foreigner as to customs and manners of the writer's country, with essay-like comment, anecdotal narrative and reminiscence rather than more extended storytelling, with humor rather than impassioned attack, and a personal tone. The sketch of manners attempts to preserve what is picturesque and characteristic that formal history neglects. Here is a link with modern oral history. The role of narrative, the impassioned attack, the extension of events in the slaughterhouse to a view of Argentina's history under Rosas—these features of "The Slaughterhouse" distinguish it from the "Apology of the Brisket."

The humor of the "Apology of the Brisket" is much lighter than the biting sarcasm of parts of "The Slaughterhouse." One example: Echeverría expresses the hope that he can preserve this example of national spirit by recourse to the press (as intellectual godmother) to help in the delivery of the essay without the aid of forceps (V, 202). There is seriousness of purpose; Larra's sketches are to be transferred to Argentina through the pen of Echevería. Argentina's "matambre" or "brisket" is shown to bear comparison with the Englishman's roast beef and plum pudding, the Italian's macaroni, the Frenchman's omelettes, the Spaniard's olla podrida. (V, 202). There is a glimpse of the writer's childhood, when he was taken by his mother to the country for a stroll—carriages were rare in those days—and they visited a country estate. The child was asked by his mother to go play with the other children, and when he displayed reluctance, a beautiful woman at the estate interceded and placed the lad at the table with the adults for lunch. She asked him whether he wanted the brisket fat or lean, and he replied that he wanted it fat and lean and sticking together, to the amusement of all and the delight of the charming woman who bestowed a hearty and affectionate kiss on the child (V, 206). This is a playful and graceful writing, with some elements to be found in "The Slaughterhouse," but remains an uncomplicated example of the true sketch of manners.

The second composition mentioned by Ghiano was not published until Gutiérrez included it in the complete works, together with other posthumous ones. It is a fragment, clearly designated as an introduction. The title is "Historia de un matambre de toro" (V, 374–381) ("History of a Bull's Brisket"). The title recalls the fact that Matasiete received the brisket of a bull in "The Slaughterhouse," and that this was exceptional since bull meat should be thrown away to the dogs (V, 233). Since the work as it stands is incomplete, it is barely possible that there would be a connection between the killing of the bull by Matasiete and the incompleted part of the "History of the Bull's Brisket."

More certain than this dubious connection are the references to Echeverría's literary opponent, apologist for the Rosas regime, the Neapolitan Pedro de Angelis. He speaks of "los *poliglotos* transatlánticos que por fortuna campean en nuestra literatura y a quienes deseo imitar en cuanto lo permita la escasez de mis luces; pero no lo haré como Mr. Le chevalier, 'Petrus in cunctis' sino en tiempo y lugar, y cuando me sople la musa de la erudición." (V, 377) ("the transatlantic *polyglots* who for fortune make a path in our literature and whom I desire to imitate in measure as my slight intelligence may permit; but I shall not do so like Mr. The knight, 'Peter in all (things)' but in time and place, and when the muse of erudition inspires me.") "Transatlantic" accords with Naples; "polyglots" recalls the fact that Pedro de Angelis used three languages in his *American Archive* (IV, 229) in addition to being Italian by birth; Petrus is the Latin form of Pedro. A second allusion is even clearer: ". . . el ilustre *Petrus*, cuyo profundo y laborioso ingenio después de haber ilustrado a su patria adoptiva con tanta obra singular, busca el descanso compilando su antigua y moderna historia . . ." (V, 378) (". . . the illustrious *Petrus*, whose profound and hard-working wit after having enlightened his adoptive fatherland with so many singular works, seeks rest compiling his ancient and modern history . . .") The "ancient and modern history" must be De Angelis's *Colección de documentos relativos a la historia antigua y moderna de las provincias del Río de la Plata* (1835–1837). (*Collection of Documents Relating to the Ancient and Modern History of the Provinces of the River Plate.*) The words "ancient and modern history" seem transparently allusive. Playfully Echeverría suggests that his composition is dedicated and presented to illustrious Petrus (i.e. Pedro de Angelis) with the request that it be included, if considered worthy, in his "larga y profunda compilación". ("long and profound compilation.") This he states in a sentence fourteen lines long, which he says is long, like the sentences of Pedro de Angelis, but not so profound! (V, 378). It seems likely that Echeverría felt that the editor of the *Collection of Documents* would not be eager to accept the contribution; it also seems likely that when he was writing the introduction to the "History of a Bull's Brisket" the *Collection of Documents* was in progress, so that Echeverría's fragment can be assumed to date from 1835 to 1837.

Echeverría implies that his "History of a Bull's Brisket" will be limited to individual matters, and will not be political, civil, literary, nor scientific history; he is somewhat pessimistic in suggesting that the man of his day is what he has always been, though polished customs mask man's perversity and permit the existence of evils unknown in barbaric times (V, 376). The pessimism and open personal reference to Pedro de Angelis suggest that at the time Echeverría was willing to express fairly openly displeasure with the intellectual climate of Buenos Aires under Rosas. "The Slaughterhouse" may be viewed as a culmination of this attitude. Comparisons with other short stories and with other sketches of manners are helpful but not much is gained by trying to force "The Slaughterhouse" into a specific mould. It is unique, and resembles Sarmiento's *Facundo* in not being a good example of any single genre.

Readers have access to a wide variety of editions, even to translations into English, complete and incomplete, of "The Slaughterhouse," which is unusual for works by Echeverría. A fairly recent book includes it for students of Spanish in a textbook with notes and vocabulary, edited by Daniel R. Reedy and Joseph R. Jones.[26] A modern anthology edited by Emir Rodríguez Monegal includes an English version, which has also been published separately, by Angel Flores.[27] Fleur Cowles provided a paraphrase and translation of the final climactic episode of the Unitarian in an absorbing book, in which historical parallels between Juan Domingo Perón and Evita Perón on the one hand, and Juan Manuel de Rosas and Encarnación Ezcurra de Rosas on the other are drawn with journalistic expertise.[28]

CHAPTER 7

A PROSE MISCELLANY

A number of prose writings remain to be mentioned. They fall into several categories which lend themselves to separate treatment from language to autobiography.

I. Spanish Language

Presumably dating from his Paris years, when he realized that his Spanish language needed improvement, are collections of idioms and of quotations (V, 155–174). Gutiérrez says that he suppressed the greater part of these lists, but that he included a sampling in order to show the conscientious effort on the poet's part to learn from the masters of the Spanish language of the sixteenth and seventeenth centuries; he refers to Antonio de Capmany's *Teatro histórico-crítico de la elocuencia española. (Historico-critical Theater of Spanish Eloquence)*. The first list is an alphabetically arranged list of idiomatic expressions like "echar margaritas a puercos" ("to throw pearls before swine") sometimes with an indication as to author. The second list is of complete quotations, many of them from the writings of Diego de Saavedra Fajardo, famous Spanish diplomat and essayist of the seventeenth century. Roberto F. Giusti has suggested that a patient study might permit students to discover how many of these expressions and idioms were later used by Echeverría, and that the results of such a study would be of value in analyzing Echeverría's style.[1] One of the quotations is used in the "Apology of the brisket" (V, 202): "Antonio Pérez decía: 'sólo los grandes estómagos digieren veneno' y yo digo: sólo los grandes estómagos digieren matambre." ("Antonio Pérez used to say: 'only great stomachs digest poison' and I say: only great stomachs digest brisket.") The Pérez quotation is found in the third volume of Capmany's *Historico-critical Theater of Spanish Eloquence* on page 552, from a letter to the Constable of France, the Duke of Montmorency, dated November 10, 1601. (See BAE, XIII 493 for the letter in question.) The quotation is not of importance, but this is an example showing that at least some of this notetaking was later used by Echeverría in his writing.

II. Education

Much of Echeverría's work in the field of pure education is related to his appointment as member of the Institute of Public Instruction in Montevideo in 1846.

Perhaps Echeverría's speech entitled "Mayo y la enseñanza popular en el Plata" (IV, 208–227) ("May and popular instruction in the Plate [region]") was a factor in this appointment. The speech was prepared for delivery at a celebration of Argentina's independence in Montevideo on May 25, 1844, but not delivered. The text was sent to Don Andrés Lamas, Minister of Finance of Uruguay. In it is discussed the relationship between the principles of the May Revolution and the social regeneration of Uruguay and of Argentina as well as the needs of education of the people on the basis of democracy and brotherhood. He stresses what the two countries have in common. As an example opposed to the Bacchanalian inaugural festivities of Rosas he adduces the speech of Daniel Webster on the significance of the newly erected monument at Bunker Hill in Boston before an ecstatic audience (IV, 216–217 and 420).

Echeverría's main work in the textbook field is the *Manual de enseñanza moral para las escuelas primarias del Estado Oriental* (IV, 327–411). (*Manual of Moral Instruction for the Primary Schools of Uruguay*). Interestingly enough, a special edition of this text arranged for use in Mexican schools by Francisco Sosa (1848–1925) was printed in 1892 in San Francisco. The speech on "May and popular instruction in the Plate [region]" is attached to this work as a coda (IV, 412–430). After the formal introduction the work is divided into six chapters: duties toward one's self, one's neighbor, the family, the fatherland, humanity, with a final one on moral perfection. Certain ideas of Echeverría lead him to include certain matters in the text, as he explains in his prologue. He warns against the overemphasis on medicine and law at the University of Buenos Aires, and tries to inculcate respect for work in the young students, work which may be adapted to local needs and industry. Echeverría gives the teacher some hints; he recommends oral instruction with the use of pictures and examples as well as explanation. Instruction should be reinforced by dictation, so that various senses may be used in the learning process. Instruction should be oral and simultaneous. He also speaks of the importance of the home, and particularly of the mother, in moral instruction and says that Alexis de Tocqueville attributed the prosperity and strength of the institutions of the United States to the superiority of its women. He feels that the women of his region should be equal to American women and have a deep influence on the reform of national customs and the well-being of the homeland (IV, 330–344).

A short book review in his "Informe presentado . . . al Instituto de Instrucción Pública sobre 'Elementos de lectura' del Doctor Don Luis J. de la Peña" (V, 386–393) ("Report presented . . . to the Institute of Public Instruction on 'Elements of Reading' by Dr. Luis J. de la Peña"). Echeverría points out that the book is the result of long study and experience in the teaching of reading on the part of its author. In the book, letters are presented together with pictures that suggest words beginning with sounds corresponding to the appropriate letters. Combinations of letters make use only of letters previously learned; practice in writing is also introduced, thus incorporating oral and written aspects of instruction. After the elements are presented, the reading exercises include elementary notions of moral and religious instruction, which Echeverría approves. This report, dated 27 November 1847, was submitted to Don Manuel Herrera y Obes, President of the Institute of Public Instruction.

Another fragmentary work, "Objeto y fines de la instrucción pública," (V, 394–402) ("Object and goals of public instruction") is addressed to the Council on Public Instruction of Montevideo. In the part completed, the author suggests that the times require something different from earlier forms of public instruction and points out that in France governments have recognized the need to adapt the educational system to interest of the rulers. He also refers to advances in science and education in Germany, but says that imitation of Germany is not the course for democracies; needs both of the countryside and of the cities must be recognized. He also senses the need for articulation between primary and secondary education, of which university education should be a harmonious continuation.

Echeverría also makes an "Análisis de la siguiente obra, The training system, established in the Glasgow normal seminary, and the model schools, by David Stow" (V, 403–406) ("Analysis of the following work . . .") The child begins learning by a method both simultaneous and oral; a child of five or six years after two or three years in school under this method can readily read a chapter from the New Testament, without having had a book in his hand in the classroom. Question and answer and oral practice come before reference is made to the textbook. The Stow system was developed first in a Sunday school; by 1835 and 1836 it had been adopted as the basis for the normal seminary by the Glasgow Society of Education. Three quarters of the work done by students can be done without the teacher's intervention. Gutiérrez points out that in a part not included by him, Echeverría transcribed sentences from the book in the original English, without translation.

III. History

On July 22, 1848 Echeverría sent to the editor of *El Conservador* in Montevideo for publication his "Revolución de febrero en Francia" (IV, 431–461) ("Revolution in February in France"). The occasion for this work was the February, 1848 revolution in which King Louis Philippe was forced to abdicate and leave France. Other revolutions or insurrections took place in western Europe in fairly rapid succession. Echeverría feels that this revolution is certain to have an effect in Hispanic America; France will lead the way, just as it did in the wars of independence. In view of the importance of this revolution for the future of Hispanic America, Echeverría has decided to subject events to an analysis. The New World can utilize much of the French experience although the circumstances of society in Hispanic America are different from those of France. The New World should not blindly imitate the Old World. Even what is good in Europe is not necessarily good for the Americas. In this connection, Echeverría quotes from the *Socialist Dogma* his reservations about accepting European thought (IV, 438–439 from IV, 193–194). A second part of the analysis deals with the "Sentido filosófico de la revolución de febrero en Francia" (IV, 439–461) ("Philosophical Meaning of the February Revolution in France"). In this section, Echeverría shows knowledge of the thought of French thinkers like Pierre Leroux and concepts of perfectibility, progress, reason, exploitation, and the proletariat. He refers to the workers of Lyons who took part in a labor insurrection in April of 1834 with the motto, "To live working or to die fighting!" (IV, 451). According to Echeverría, fraternity is the way in which the regeneration of the free peoples of the world may be realized. He intended to complete this historical study with two more sections, one on the historical, political, and social meaning of the revolution, and the other on the historic parallels between France and Argentina.

Two other works treat aspects of Argentina's history: "Antecedentes y primeros pasos de la Revolución de Mayo" (V, 243–266) ("Antecedents and first steps of the Revolution of May") and the fragmentary "Origen y naturaleza de los poderes extraordinarios acordados a Rosas" (V, 267–308) ("Origin and nature of the extraordinary powers granted to Rosas"). In the former, after setting the background of a backward Spain and an even more backward New World group of Spanish colonies, he divides American society into groups: 1.) the clergy, the toga wearers, and the bosses; 2.) those made wealthy by monopoly and fortune; 3.) the rustics known as *gauchos* and *compadritos* in the River Plate region, besides the indigenous and African groups, slaves and outside the main society. The first three groups correspond to the aristocracy, the middle class, and the manual laborers (artisans and proletariats). The revolution came from the first two groups, educated and familiar with the writings of writers like Montesquieu, Rousseau, and the Encyclopedists of France. He narrates events from the British invasions of 1806 and 1807 in Buenos Aires to the establishment of a junta animated by the revolutionary spirit of Mariano Moreno.

The second work is composed of fragments, but deals with such matters as the detrimental effects of the law of March 7, 1835, in which extraordinary powers were given to Rosas, the type of constitution which had existed prior to that time, and the tyranny and usurpation of Rosas. Echeverría has scorn for those who would compare Rosas with Cato, Cincinnatus, or George Washington (V, 289). In his words: "Washington fue el héroe de la independencia americana y uno de los fundadores de su constitución, Rosas un caudillo vulgar, formado de la escoria inmunda de la anarquía y que no dejará a su país más que recuerdos de sangre, exterminio y mengua" (V, 289–290). ("Washington was the hero of American independence and one of the founders of their constitution, Rosas an ordinary caudillo, formed by the foul scum of anarchy and who will not leave to his country anything other than memories of blood, extermination, and decline.")

IV. Literary Criticism

Probably the best examples of Echeverría's literary criticism are in his statements of artistic purpose written in connection with such works as "The Consolations" and "The Captive Woman." It is probably best to consider the various writings included by Gutiérrez in the fifth volume of the collected works as notes in which his own ideas are not clearly differentiated from those he may have wished to quote or to paraphrase. These include ideas taken from such sources as Hugo's preface to *Cromwell*.[2]

V. Economics

Gutiérrez places under the heading of political economy a fragment entitled "La contribución territorial" (V, 353–356) ("The territorial contribution.") He contrasts the land situation of Argentina with that of England and France; fertility of land is not something that can be used as a factor in the former country for determining land taxes, since Argentina's lands are generally fertile. Production must be a basis for differentiation. Also distance from the city must be a factor, because of transportation costs. In this fragment Echeverría clearly shows that he has taken into consideration Argentina's conditions and not tried to adopt systems developed in other places for his own country.

VI. Philosophy

An example of a philosophical writing preserved is called "Sistemas" (V, 370–373) ("Systems"). This is believed by the compiler to be part of a serious examination of philosophical systems, especially that of Franz Joseph Gall, on the basis of data that led him to think so.

VII. Speeches

Gutiérrez gathers together several speeches or lectures connected with the Literary Salon and the Association of May. The titles are: "Discurso de introducción a una serie de lecturas pronunciadas en el 'Salón Literario' en setiembre de 1837" (V, 309–336) ("Introductory speech to a series of readings delivered in the 'Literary Salon' in September, 1837"); "Segunda lectura," (V, 337–352) ("Second Reading"); "Exposiciones hechas en el seno de la Asociación 'Mayo' " (V, 357–369) ("Expositions made at the headquarters of the 'May' Association"). In the first one he characterizes the era and state of intellectual culture in Argentina in 1837 (or 1836, since he refers to twenty-six years of political life for Argentina) (V, 334).

The second selection has gaps, but puts into focus industry, including the work of artisans, and work on the land. The third selection includes the startling announcement that indiscretion has betrayed the Association to Rosas, and the expression of Echeverría's willingness to scrap the Code (or Credo or Dogma) if any member of the Association can formulate something better. It concludes with Echeverría's words at the last meeting in which he expresses the hope that with the appearance of the new sun of May, all the members may join together in the ranks of liberators and regenerators of the fatherland.

VIII. Autobiography

It is impossible to read Echeverría's works without being impressed by the degree to which true or literary autobiography seems to be part of their composition. Two sections in the fifth volume of Gutiérrez's edition of the complete works repay the reader interested in Echeverría's life, but there is a possibility that they reflect the actuality only partially or in a literary way. They reveal and conceal, sometimes at the same time. One is the "Letters to a friend" (V, 20–73) and the other has as heading "Pensamientos, ideas, opiniones, rasgos autobiográficos, párrafos de correspondencia epistolar, etc," (V, 430–458) ("Thoughts, ideas, opinions, autobiographical sketches, paragraphs of epistolary correspondence, etc,") One more prose work which does not fit neatly into any category is the "Mefistófeles, drama joco-serio, satírico-político" (V, 180–199) ("Mephistopheles, jocose-serious, satirico-political drama"). It is not a play, and is narrated in the first person. At one moment in the narrative, Echeverría says that he feels like translating a passage from Goethe's *Faust*. It may be that his translation of the prologue of that work should be inserted at this point into the "Mephistopheles" (III, 302–304 to be inserted at V, 192) At this moment, Echeverría, like Faust before him, is visited by a Mephistophelian figure.

There remain fascinating puzzles in the interpretation of the posthumously published works; their elucidation should be a stimulus to readers for years to come. If the insertion of the translation in this case is considered to be appropriate, it may be that further rearrangement and piecing together parts and fragments may shed light, not only on Echeverría's techniques, but also on works like "The Slaughterhouse" which have called forth such variety of interpretation.

CHAPTER 8

ECHEVERRÍA'S POSITION IN LITERATURE

European Romanticism strongly influenced Echeverría at least in part because of his stay in Paris when that movement was at its height. He became familiar there with German and English literatures, some probably through French translations. Writers like Byron, the Romantics of France and of Germany, exerted an influence on him that cannot be denied. The influence of a writer like Shakespeare seems to have been direct and, in some cases, indirect.

His connections with music are important; he was an adept performer on the guitar, and this may have contributed to the musicality of his verse. His collaboration with the composers of Argentina of his day, particularly with Juan Pedro Esnaola, as a songwriter is noteworthy.

His knowledge of Italian and of older Spanish literature had a secure basis. Although he has been denounced for hostility to the literature of Spain, this is not true with regard to the Golden Age writers, and he shows respect for such writers of the nineteenth century as Quintana and Larra, and may even have taken a motif for one of his poems from the relatively obscure Father Arolas.

He displays knowledge of American writers like Daniel Webster and Washington Irving, and of Spanish American poets like Cuba's Heredia. He also uses epigraphs from Portugal's great epic poem *Os Lusíadas (The Lusíads)* of Camoëns.

His work shows knowledge of Greek and Roman literature; he even takes an epigraph from the Aeneid.[1]

The Bible also appears to have influenced his style in his prose, particularly in the *Socialist Dogma,* as well as having inspired some poems of religious, philosophical tone.

These influences were assimilated thoroughly in to his introspective and autobiographical inspiration. He is Romanticist as poet and also in his fate-tossed life. Precarious health, the fight against tyranny, years in exile, loves intense and tinged with a melancholy strain are aspects of life that did not require Echeverría to search his imagination.

His idealism and energy are appealing qualities. Reading and life are revealed, sometimes ambiguously but in abundance, in his prose and poetry. They have left an indelible impression.

Carlos M. Urien has called Echeverría the incarnation of thought for his country's literature and politics for the last two decades of his life.[2] He never let his thought be bridled by the dictatorship of Rosas, and even in exile kept on representing the intellectual ideals of Argentina or of May.

Echeverría's Romanticism was not merely the introduction to a new environment of a literary movement or of an alien philosophy. He constantly fought to adapt ideas to Argentina's needs and stage of development. In literature, he exploited the natural environment of his homeland; he glorified its history, the sacrifices of the martyrs for independence and for freedom, their patriotism. For Echeverría these themes were principles to live by. His unhappy exile was due to the conviction that Rosas's rule was evil.

Echeverría continued the traditions of older poets of Argentina in his patriotic verse, and greatly increased the range of its literature by his narrative poems in the Romantic tradition, by his varied and intimate lyricism and by his concern with the setting, the pampa, the great river, and the social life.

His contibution as mentor to young intellectuals in Buenos Aires in fomenting liberalism and in keeping alive opposition to Rosas was great. He had an interest in the past (the ideals of the Revolution of May of 1810) and hope in the future (when true democracy would result in a regenerated Argentina with the end of Rosas's tyranny). The Socialist Dogma is a masterpiece of this facet of Echeverría's thought.

José Mármol, poet and novelist, owes much to Echeverría.[3] He referred to him as a poetic nightingale (Juicios críticos, V, xlvi).

In dealing with the countryside Echeverría is an initiator in the tradition attracting other leading nineteenth century poets like José Hernández, author of the gaucho masterpiece, *Martín Fierro*.

His masterpiece, "The Slaughterhouse," continues to fascinate readers and critics who respond positively to its vigor and sincerity.

As literary critic, Echeverría's contribution is solid. He emphasized the need for literature in Argentina to be Christian, liberal, American, and Argentinian.[4] Echeverría, too, has become part of Hispanic literature, not only for what he wrote, but also for use made of him as a figure in literary works written years after his death.

A few days after Echeverría's death in exile in Montevideo Rafael Obligado was born in Buenos Aires, one of the most respected poets of Argentina in the later years of the century. The date was January 27, 1851. About thirty years later Obligado composed a poem entitled "Echeverría," characterized as the manifesto of the Academia Argentina or Argentinian Academy, a literary society which sought to nationalize their literature on the model of "The Captive Woman." The key words of this poem by Obligado are "Lancémonos nosotros sus hermanos/Por la senda inmortal de Echeverría".[5] ("Let us his brothers rush along the immortal path of Echeverría.") Nine years before the composition of "Echeverría" another fine poem was composed by Obligado, "La pampa," ("The Pampa") which pays tribute to Echeverría and even recalls one of the similes of "The Captive Woman."[6] Yet another poem by Obligado, "América", ("America") brings into verse again the noble "captive woman" and her beloved Brian.[7] Quite consciously, Obligado desired to wear Echeverría's mantle.

The imagination of a leading writer in Spain of the first half of the twentieth century, Azorín, was fired by Echeverría. Both men, poets in Spanish, spent time in Paris. Azorín was fond of evoking the past, and in 1937 in Paris wrote a parable called "Echeverría y el cristal" ("Echeverría and glass").[8] This was a work descriptive of what might have happened, but did not.

Poems by Echeverría are woven into the frame of the sketch, which seems to transport Echeverría to Azorín's own day. He is depicted as a man of the sea, a great poet; his muse is of remembrance and sorrow. His verse are spoken of as transparent; this is credited to the poet's belief that he is (like a Cervantes creation) made of glass. Azorín shows admiration for his poems and the parable may be read as literary criticism. It may be more significant in this study in showing the appeal exerted by Echevería's life and personality as well as his works through the years; his presence in this work by Azorín makes him definitely a figure of Spain's literature.

Less surprising, but also of interest, is the inclusion of Echeverría as a character in the series of historical novels on the Rosas era by Argentina's Manuel Gálvez, works written after considerable careful research. Between 1931 and 1954 were published seven novels in the series and also a biography of Rosas by Gálvez. He desired to rectify what he felt was a falsely negative view of Rosas by stressing the debt Argentina and its people owed to that leader.

Echeverría's life in Buenos Aires is part of *La ciudad pintada de rojo (The City Painted Red),* which appeared in 1948; in this novel the fictional Rita Claustro falls in love with him. Other characters include Pedro de Angelis and Juan María Gutiérrez.

Echeverría's exile in Montevideo is featured in *Bajo la garra anglofrancesa (Under the Anglo-French Claw),* published in 1952. Here Echeverría is a friend of the fictional Prudente Wells. The three most famous literary attackers of Rosas all make their appearance in *Under the Anglo-French Claw:* Echeverría, Sarmiento, and José Mármol.

Gálvez permits his view of Echeverría as political thinker to be glimpsed through remarks made by Wells to the poet. For him Echeverría desired the rule of an intellectual aristocracy and was no democrat. Wells hinted, too, that he found it a bore to listen to verses from *The Fallen Angel.*[9]

About a generation later appeared a play inspired by Echeverría and Mariquita Sánchez, mother of his friend, Juan Thompson, hostess of probably the most famous Buenos Aires salon.[10]

There is, thus, evidence of the lasting appeal of the poet as a colorful figure. Admiration is not universal; those who admire Rosas, have little affection for Echeverría, and the reverse tends to be true.

Still, it seems just to conclude this study with the following comprehensive statement: "Esteban Echeverría remains almost unrivaled as molder of Argentine national spirit; every later generation has rediscovered him for itself and found in his writings inspirations and reinforcement for its own Argentine idealism, nationalism, and identity."[11]

NOTES AND REFERENCES

ABBREVIATIONS

AnEA	Anuario de estudios americanos
APHA	Antología de poetas hispanoamericanos
BAAL	Boletín de la Academia Argentina de Letras
BAE	Biblioteca de autores españoles
CA	Cuadernos americanos
GEA	Gran enciclopedia argentina
HDA	Historical Dictionary of Argentina
Hisp	Hispania
HMA	Historia de la música en la Argentina, 1536–1851
IARB	Inter-American Review of Bibliography
LALR	Latin-American Literary Review
OC	Obras completas
REH	Revista de estudios hispánicos
RHM	Revista hispánica moderna
RI	Revista iberoamericana
RN	Romance Notes
SSF	Studies in Short Fiction

Chapter One

1. John W. White, *Argentina, The Life Story of a Nation*, New York, 1942, p. 76.
2. Ibid., p. 77.
3. Ibid., p. 78.
4. Ernesto J.A. Maeder, *Evolución demográfica argentina desde 1810 a 1869*, Buenos Aires, 1969, p. 34.
5. Hubert Herring, *A History of Latin America from the Beginnings to the Present*, New York, 1961, p. 614.
6. *The World Almanac & Book of Facts*, 1978, p. 513.
7. Herring, *History of Latin America*, p. 614.
8. James R. Scobie, *Argentina, a City and a Nation*, New York, 1964, pp. 31–32.
9. Inés Muñoz, tr., Domingo Faustino Sarmiento, *Travels, A Selection*, Washington, D.C., 1963, p. 34.
10. Ibid., p. 35.
11. Kempton E. Webb, *Geography of Latin America*, Englewood Cliffs, New Jersey, 1972, pp. 79–82 and 86.
12. Miron Burgin, "Rosas Assured the Continued Prosperity of the Pastoral Industries," quoted from Lewis Hanke, ed., *History of Latin American Civilization, Sources and Interpretation*, Boston, 1973, II, 93.

Chapter Two

1. Angel J. Battistessa, ed., Esteban Echeverría, *La cautiva, El matadero*, Buenos Aires, 1958, pp. lxxx and xix.
2. Ernesto Morales, *Esteban Echeverría*, Buenos Aires, 1950, p. 28.
3. Noé Jitrik, *Esteban Echeverría*, Buenos Aires, 1967, p. 7.
4. Esteban Echeverría, OC, Buenos Aires, 1874, V, iv. Further references as indicated.
5. Jitrik, *Esteban Echeverría*, p. 8; Alberto Placos, ed., Esteban Echeverría, *Dogma socialista*, La Plata, 1940, p. ix.
6. Delia S. Etcheverry, ed., Domingo Faustino Sarmiento, *Facundo*, Buenos Aires, 1940, p. 69.
7. Gilbert Chase, *The Music of Spain*, New York, 1941, p. 221 for Dionisio Aguado and Fernando Sor.
8. Etcheverry, *Facundo*, p. 69.
9. Battistessa, *La cautiva, El matadero*, p. xix.
10. Palcos, *Dogma socialista*, p. xi.
11. Ibid., p. xii.
12. Ibid., p. xii.
13. Ibid., p. xii.
14. Battistessa, *La cautiva, El matadero*, pp. xxiv, lxxxiii.
15. In chronological order: William Shakespeare (1564–1616), Johann Wolfgang von Goethe (1749–1832), Friedrich von Schiller (1759–1805), and George Gordon Lord Byron (1788–1824).
16. These French thinkers are Blaise Pascal (1623–1662), Charles-Louis de Secondat, Baron de Montesquieu (1689–1755), François Guizot (1787–1874), Victor Cousin (1792–1867), and Pierre Leroux (1797–1871).
17. Battistessa, *La cautiva, El matadero*, p. xxvii.
18. Nydia Lamarque, *Echeverría el poeta*, Buenos Aires, 1951, p. 44.
19. Morales, *Esteban Echeverría*, p. 75.
20. Vicente Gesualdo, HMA, Buenos Aires, 1961, I, 453.
21. Ibid., pp. 482–489. See also Guillermo Gallardo, *Juan Pedro Esnaola, una estirpe musical*, Buenos Aires, 1960, pp. 95–100, songs numbered 5, 8, 9, 11, 13, 14, 17, 19, 21.
22. Morales, *Esteban Echeverría*, pp. 81–83.
23. Ibid., p. 84.
24. F(élix) W(einberg), in *Enciclopedia de la literatura argentina*, directed by Pedro Orgambide and Roberto Yahni, Buenos Aires, 1970, pp. 555–556.
25. Battistessa, *La cautiva, El matadero*, pp. xxxii-xxxiii, and Alfredo L. Palacios, *Estevan Echeverría, albacea del pensamiento de Mayo*, Buenos Aires, 1955, p. 387.
26. Battistessa, *La cautiva, El matadero*, p. xxxiv.
27. Ibid., p. xxxiv.
28. Ibid., p. xxxiv.

29. José Luis Lanuza, *Echeverría y sus amigos*, Buenos Aires, 1967, pp. 177–185.
30. Muñoz, *Travels*, pp. 69–70.
31. Morales, *Esteban Echeverría*, pp. 209, 212–213.
32. Jitrik, *Esteban Echeverría*, pp. 51–52; Morales, *Esteban Echeverría*, pp. 215–217. V, "Juicios críticos," cxlix, cliii.

Chapter Three

1. Theodore Andersson, *Carlos María Ocantos, Argentine Novelist, A study of Indigenous French and Spanish Elements in His Work*, New Haven, 1934, p. 4; on page 29, Andersson points out that the call to Americanization is "positive in that it urges the cultivation of the new individuality of the region, and negative in that it repudiates all foreign influence."
2. This passage is a translation from Amédée Pichot's *Voyage historique et littéraire en Angleterre et en Ecosse*, II, 413 and 403, as pointed out by Rafael Alberto Arrieta, "Esteban Echeverría y el Romanticismo en el Plata," in his *Historia de la literatura argentina*, Buenos Aires, 1958, II, 97.
3. Buenaventura Carlos Aribau, ed., *Obras de D. Nicolás y de D. Leandro Fernández de Moratín*, in BAE, Madrid, 1944, II, 19.
4. *The Complete Poetical Works of William Wordsworth*, Boston, New York, etc., 1904, p. 256.
5. James Willis Posey, "Byron and Echeverría," Master of Arts thesis University of North Carolina 1927, p. 76.
6. Pedro Henríquez Ureña, *Literary Currents in Hispanic America*, Cambridge, Massachusetts, 1949, pp. 117–118, 243–244.
7. Eduardo Joubin Colombres, "La vocación poética de Echeverría, " in Esteban Echeverría, OC, Buenos Aires, 1951, p. 564.
8. Ibid., p. 566.
9. Morales, *Esteban Echeverría*, pp. 69–72.
10. Juan Eugenio Hartzenbusch, ed., *Obras de Calderón de la Barca*, BAE, Madrid, 1944, VII, 16. Calderón's *La vida es sueño*, III, x.
11. William Sharp, ed., James Macpherson, *Poems of Ossian*, Edinburgh, 1896, p. 345.
12. Lamarque, *Echeverría el poeta*, pp. 17, 38.
13. Gutiérrez (III, 143), however, gives "La ida" ("The departure").
14. Ernest Hartley Coleridge, ed., *The Works of Lord Byron, Poetry*, London, 1904, III, 157.
15. Calvin Thomas, *A History of German Literature*, New York, 1909, p. 326.
16. See David William Foster, "A Note on Espronceda's Use of the Romance Meter in *El Estudiante de Salamanca*," RN, 7 (1965), 16–20.

17. Etcheverry, *Facundo*, pp. 61–62.
18. Peter G. Earle, *Prophet in the Wilderness, The Works of Ezequiel Martínez Estrada*, Austin and London, 1971, pp. 9–10.
19. Ezequiel Martínez Estrada, *Muerte y transfiguración de Martín Fierro*, Mexico, Buenos Aires, 1958, II, 396.
20. GEA, Buenos Aires, 1956, II, s. v. *cautivo*.
21. Lucio Victoria Mansilla, *Una excursión a los indios ranqueles*, Buenos Aires, 1870, II, 34, cited from the source of note 20.
22. Jorge Luis Borges, OC, Buenos Aires, 1974, p. 788.
23. For the tradition of the *cautiva*, see David Lagmanovich, "Tres cautivas: Echeverría, Ascasubi, Hernández," in *Chasqui*, 8 (1979), 24–33.
24. Edgar C. Knowlton, Jr., "The Epigraphs in Esteban Echeverría's 'La Cautiva," in Hisp, 44 (1961), 212–217.
25. Ibid., p. 214.
26. Victor Hugo, *Les Orientales*, 1880, p. 40b: "Mazeppa."
27. The translation is from E. Herman Hespelt, ed., *An Anthology of Spanish American Literature*, New York, 1946, p. 172. Changes to *orribili* and *Facevano* will make the text agree with Charles S. Singleton, rev. Charles H. Grandgent, ed., Dante Alighieri, *La divina commedia*, Cambridge, Massachusetts, 1972, p. 29. From *Inferno*, III, 25–28.
28. Hartzenbusch, *Obras de Calderón*, BAE, VII, 219.
29. Giuseppe Lipparini, ed., *I grandi autori della letteratura italiana*, Milan, 1945, III, 30.
30. Singleton, *La divina commedia*, p. 79. *Inferno*, VIII, 106–107.
31. Luis Fernández-Guerra y Orbe, ed., *Comedias escogidas de D. Agustín Moreto y Cabaña*, Madrid, 1950, BAE, XXXIX, 515. From *La confusión de un jardín*.
32. Alphonse de Lamartine, *Nouvelles méditations poétiques*, bound together with *Le Dernier Chant du pèlerinage d'Harold* and the *Chant du sacre*, Paris, 1892, p. 249.
33. Alphonse de Lamartine, *Oeuvres complètes*, Paris, 1861, VIII, 46–47 and 362. This volume corresponds to the third of his *Voyage en Orient, 1832–1833*.
34. Alessandro D'Ancona and Orazio Bacci, *Manuale della letteratura italiana*, Florence, 1928, I, 532.
35. Letter to the author from Roberto F. Giusti, dated 1 March 1966 at Martínez.
36. Alphonse de Lamartine, *Premières méditations poétiques*, Paris, 1891, p. 28, in the poem "Le Soir" ("The Evening").
37. Carlos M. Urien, *Esteban Echeverría, ensayo crítico-histórico sobre su vida y obras con motivo de la erección de su estatua*, Buenos Aires, 1905, pp. 35–36.
38. Etcheverry, *Facundo*, pp. 64–65.
39. Battistessa, *La cautiva, El matadero*, p. lxxxix.

40. The passage occurs in Martin de Moussy's work, I, Paris, 1860, beginning with page 242.
41. Héctor Roberto Baudón, *Echeverría, Mármol*, Buenos Aires, 1918, p. 41.
42. José Cantarell Dart, prologue to Juan María Gutiérrez, *Letras argentinas*, Buenos Aires, New York, etc., n.d., p. xix.
43. Morales, *Esteban Echeverría*, pp. 94–95.
44. Charles W. Humphreys, tr., Esteban Echeverría, *The Captive Woman*, Buenos Aires, 1905, p. 15.
45. Ibid., p. 23.
46. H. H. Vaughan and M. A. de Vitis, ed., Antonio García Gutiérrez, *El trovador*, Boston, New York, etc., 1930, p. 76.
47. Ibid., p. 78; Rodolfo A. Borello, "Notas a *La Cautiva*," in *Logos*, 13–14 (1977–78), 82–84.
48. Jean Franco, *A Literary History of Spain: Spanish American Literature since Independence*, London, New York, 1973, p. 41.
49. Etcheverry, *Facundo*, pp. 127–129. General Juan Facundo Quiroga, beset by a *tigre*, "tiger," stated: "Entonces supe lo que era tener miedo." ("Then I learned what it was to be afraid.")
50. Martínez Estrada, *Muerte y transfiguración de Martín Fierro*, II, 396.
51. Enrique Williams Alzaga, *La pampa en la novela argentina*, Buenos Aires, 1955, p. 93.
52. Martin S. Stabb, *Jorge Luis Borges*, New York, 1970, p. 63.
53. Borges, OC, p. 270.
54. Manuel García Puertas, *El romanticismo de Esteban Echeverría*, Montevideo, 1957, pp. 24–25.
55. "Juicios críticos," V, lxxx-lxxxi, cxxxiii-cxxxxiv.
56. Juan Collantes de Terán, "El romanticismo en Esteban Echeverría," in AnEA (Escuela de Estudios Hispano-Americanos, Seville), 24 (1967), 1739–1783.
57. Ibid., p. 1751.
58. Ibid., pp. 1751–1755.
59. Ibid., pp. 1755–1762.
60. Ibid., pp. 1762–1766.
61. Ibid., p. 1766.
62. Ibid., p. 1775.
63. Ibid., p. 1776.
64. Ibid., p. 1777.
65. Ibid., pp. 1779–1783.
66. Ione S. Wright and Lisa M. Nekhom, HDA, Metuchen, London, 1978, p. 160.
67. Ibid., p. 227.
68. Ibid., p. 779.
69. Santillán, GEA, IV, s.v. Domingo Lastra.
70. Wright and Nekhom, HDA, pp. 756–757.

71. Palacios, *Estevan Echeverría*, p. 354.
72. Wright and Nekhom, HDA, pp. 654–655. The family name was properly Rozas, but the dictator used the spelling Rosas after leaving home. See Santillán, GEA, VII, 253.
73. Gordon C. Lee, ed., *Crusade Against Ignorance, Thomas Jefferson on Education*, New York, 1961, p. 31.
74. Wright and Nekhom, HDA, pp. 14–.16.
75. Joubin Colombres, "La vocación poética de Echeverría," pp. 578–580.
76. Wright and Nekhom, HDA, pp. 86–87.
77. Ibid., pp. 584–586.
78. Ibid., pp. 74–75.
79. Posey, "Byron and Echeverría," p. 53. For the opening of "The Bride of Abydos," see *The Poetical Works of Lord Byron*, London, 1926, p. 258.
80. For "Mignon," from Goethe's *Wilhelm Meisters Lehrjahre*, see Clarence Willis Eastman, ed., *Goethe's Poems*, New York, 1941, pp. 46 and 155.
81. Roberto F. Giusti, ed., Esteban Echeverría, *Prosa literaria*, Buenos Aires, 1944, p. xv.
82. Lamarque, *Echeverría el poeta*, p. 184.
83. Ibid., p. 184.
84. George Lyman Kittredge, ed., *Sixteen Plays of Shakespeare*, Boston, 1946, p. 30. The Tempest, III, iii.
85. Ibid., p. 15. *The Tempest*, I, ii.
86. Jitrik, *Esteban Echeverría*, p. 38.
87. "Juicios críticos," V, cxlvi; Posey, "Byron and Echeverría," p. 80.
88. Eugen Wildenow, ed., *Theodor Körners sämtliche Werke*, Leipzig, 1903, pp. 373–377; Lewis Melville and Reginald Hargreaves, ed., *Great German Short Stories*, New York, 1929, pp. 713–716.
89. José R. Lomba y Pedraja, *El P. Arolas, su vida y sus versos, estudio*, Madrid, 1898, p. 174, refers to "las nueve" ("nine o'clock") and says it appeared in *Poesías de D. Juan Arolas*, Valencia, 1843, III, 89. See the same scholar, ed. *Poesías del P. Arolas*, Madrid, 1949, pp. 51–61.
90. Baudón, *Echeverría, Mármol*, pp. 63–65.
91. *Poetical Works of Byron*, pp. 320–321; "Parisina" VI, VII.
92. Posey, "Byron and Echeverría," pp. 40–47.
93. Two characters of *The Fallen Angel* sing a duet from Rossini's *Otello*. (II, 337) Echeverría comments that at the time Bellini had not yet ousted Rossini from popularity in Buenos Aires.
94. Kittredge, *Sixteen Plays*, p. 1242. Othello, III, iii, 413–426.
95. Gioacchino Rossini, *Otello*, Milan, etc., n.d., p. 186. The Italian words are "Amato ben!"
96. For parallels, see Kittredge, *Sixteen Plays*, pp. 1250, 1256. 1256; *Othello*, IV, ii, 42–.43; V, ii, 37–38; V, ii, 43–45.

97. Marcelino Menéndez Pelayo, *Historia de la poesía argentina*, Buenos Aires, etc., 1947, p. 111.
98. Jitrik, Esteban Echeverría, p. 48.
99. Ibid., p. 49.
100. Posey, "Byron and Echeverría," pp. 83–93.
101. Ibid., p. 85.
102. Ibid., p. 88.
103. Ibid., p. 89.
104. Ibid., p. 92.
105. Alexandre Dumas, *Angèle*, Paris, n.d., p. 13. II, ii.
106. Raúl H. Castagnino, *El teatro en Buenos Aires durante la época de Rosas*, Buenos Aires, 1944, p. 638.
107. Ibid., p. 34.
108. Ibid., p. 501.
109. Ibid., p. 504.
110. Personal letter from Raúl H. Castagnino, dated 2 August 1977 at Buenos Aires.
111. Gesualdo, HMA, I, 553.
112. Baudón, *Echeverría, Mármol*, p. 73.
113. Urien, *Esteban Echeverría, p. 30.*
114. Alberto Palcos, *Historia de Echeverría*, Buenos Aires, 1960, p. 156.
115. Nydia Lamarque, "El amor y los amores de Esteban Echeverría," in CA, 24 (1945), 243; García Puertas, *El romanticismo* pp. 27–28; Palacios, *Estevan Echeverría*, pp. 457–460.
116. "Juicios críticos," V, xliv-xlv; Gutiérrez comments that Echeverría forgot that art was not a photograph; for the student of society, however, photographs are desirable.
117. Morales, *Esteban Echeverría*, pp. 112–113.

Chapter Four

1. Vicente Vega, *Diccionario ilustrado de frases célebres y citas literarias*, Barcelona, 1955, p. 619, gives Catalán and Spanish texts.
2. *Poetical Works of Byron*, p. 86. from "Fare Thee Well"
3. Ibid., p. 293. From "Lara," II, III.
4. Victor Hugo, *Poésie*, Paris, n.d., I, 77. "Odes et ballades," V, x.
5. Luís de Camões, *Obras*, Oporto, 1970, p. 1310. *Os Lusíadas*, VII, lxxix, 4.
6. Posey, "Byron and Echeverría," pp. 63–67.
7. Camões, *Obras*, p. 1341. *Os Lusíadas*, IX, xii, 8.
8. François Auguste René, vicomte de Chateaubriand, *Atala, René, Le Dernier Abencérage, Les Natchez*, Paris, n.d., pp. 38–39.
9. *Poetical Works of Byron*, pp. 103–104. "Ode on Venice."

10. *La lira argentina*, Buenos Aires, c. 1924, p. 24. From the national hymn of Argentina.
11. Menéndez y Pelayo, APHA, Madrid, 1928, IV, clxviii.
12. *La lira argentina*, p. 397.
13. Juan Cruz Varela, *Poesías*, Buenos Aires, 1916, p. 102.
14. Alberto Colunga and Laurentio Turrado, ed. *Biblia sacra*, Madrid, 1965, p. 526. Psalmus 87 (88), 3, for Vulgate text.
15. Azorín, OC, Madrid, 1962, VII, 1214.
16. Colunga and Turrado, *Biblia*, p. 494, Psalmus 52 (53), 1.
17. Lamarque, *Echeverría el poeta*, p. 157.
18. Colunga and Turrado, *Biblia*, p. 460, Psalmus 16 (17), 8.
19. Ibid., p. 1190. Apocalypsis 16, 1.
20. Adolfo de Castro, ed. *Poetas líricos de los siglos xvi y xvii*, BAE, Madrid, 1950, XXXII, 381, poem by Francisco de Rioja.
21. Walter Kaufmann, ed. *Goethe's Faust*, Garden City, 1963, pp. 310–311. Part I, line 3235.
22. Ramón de Mesonero Romanos, ed. *Dramáticos posteriores a Lope de Vega*, BAE, Madrid, 1951, XLVIII, 553 from Fernando de Zárate: *Quien habla más, obra menos*, I, iv.
23. Azorín, OC, VII, 1214.
24. Menéndez y Pelayo, APHA, IV, clxviii; "Juicios críticos," V, xi–xii; Baudón, *Echeverría, Mármol*, p. 37.
25. Ernest S. Green and Miss H. von Lowenfels, tr. *Mexican and South American Poems*, New York, 1977, reprint of 1892 work.
26. Robert Southey, *The Remains of Henry Kirke White of Nottingham*, London, 1808, I, 19.
27. Fernández-Guerra y Orbe, *Comedias de Moreto*, BAE, XXXIX, 345. From *El valiente justiciero*, III, vi.
28. Kittredge, *Sixteen Plays*, p. 30. *The Tempest*, III, iii.
29. Ibid., p. 1253. *Othello*, IV, 3, 48.
30. Rossini, *Otello*, pp. 177–181.
31. Juan Eugenio Hartzenbusch, ed. Lope Félix de Vega Carpio, *Comedias escogidas*, BAE, XXXIV, 29. *La Dorotea*, III, i. Echeverría's *bellos*, "fair," corresponds to Lope's *verdes*, "green."
32. Lewis Campbell, ed. *Poems of Thomas Campbell*, London, New York, 1904, p. 26, line 373.
33. Augusto Cortina, ed. Jorge Manrique, *Cancionero*, Madrid, 1960, p. 99, lines 2073–2075. From the "Coplas."
34. Menéndez y Pelayo, APHA, IV, clxviii and "Juicios críticos," V, xv, xxx.
35. José María Heredia, *Poesías, discursos y cartas*, Havana, 1939, I, 72. For Heredia's *agostada Yace*, Echeverría has *ya agostada Siento*, with little change.
36. Hugo, *Poésie*, I, 72. *Odes et ballades*, V, i.
37. Ibid., I, 72. *Odes et ballades*, V, iv.
38. Posey, "Byron and Echeverría," pp. 68–71.

39. Lamarque, *Echeverría el poeta*, p. 20.
40. Howard Mills, ed. George Crabbe, *Tales, 1812 and Other Selected Poems*, Cambridge, 1967, p. 376, XI.
41. Morris Bishop, *A Survey of French Literature*, New York, 1965, II, 27, line 32, from Lamartine's "L'Isolement." See Azorín, OC, VII, 1214, for praise of this poem.
42. Hartzenbusch, *Obras de Calderón*, BAE, IX, 182. From *El mágico prodigioso*, II, xviii.
43. Hartzenbusch, *Obras de Calderón*, BAE, VII, 160. From *El purgatorio de San Patricio*, II, xix; *The Poetical Works of Edward Young*, Westport, 1970, I, 2. From "Night the First."
44. Lamarque, *Echeverría el poeta*, p. 21.
45. *Poetical Works of Byron*, p. 102. "Ode on Venice," II.
46. Friedrich von Schiller, *Werke*, Leipzig, n.d., IV, 330. From *Wallensteins Tod*, IV, xii, 6930–6934.
47. Ibid., II, 328. From *Kabale und Liebe* I, iv, 11–13.
48. Gesualdo, HMA, I, 552.
49. Kaufmann, *Faust*, p. 166. Part I, lines 1439–1441.
50. Riccardo Bachelli, ed. Alessandro Manzoni, *Opere*, Milan, 1953, p. 54. From *Inni sacri e odi*, III, "La risurrezione."
51. Fernández-Guerra y Orbe, *Comedias de Moreto*, BAE, XXXIX, 187. From *No puede ser*, I, i.
52. See Gabriele Rabel, *Kant*, Oxford, 1963, p. 287 and Alfred Ernest Teale, *Kantian Ethics*, London, 1951, pp. 5-6.
53. Martín García Mérou, *Ensayo sobre Echeverría*, in *Grandes escritores argentinos*, series 3, Buenos Aires, 1944, XXXIV, 240.
54. Arrieta, "Esteban Echeverría y el Romanticismo en el Plata," II, 56.
55. Lamarque, *Echeverría el poeta*, pp. 33–35, 158, 186.
56. Camões, *Obras*, p. 1345. *Os Lusíadas*, IX, xxx, 7–8.
57. Gesualdo, HMA, I, 241, 252.
58. Ibid., I, 482, 484.
59. Ibid., I, 552; Gallardo, *Juan Pedro Esnaola*, p. 96.
60. Gesualdo, HMA, I, 453, 553; Gallardo, *Juan Pedro Esnaola*, p. 96.
61. Lanuza, *Echeverría y sus amigos*, pp. 59–60.
62. Ibid., p. 61.
63. Lamarque, *Echeverría el poeta*, pp. 127–131.
64. Ibid., p. 127.
65. Gesualdo, HMA, I, 489, 568.
66. Ibid., I, 482, 553, 557; Gallardo, *Juan Pedro Esnaola*, p. 96.
67. Gesualdo, HMA, I, 484, 554.
68. Ibid., I, 488.
69. Lamarque, *Echeverría el poeta*, p. 129.
70. Alberto Williams, *Antología de compositores argentinos*, Buenos Aires, 1941, pp. 92–97.
71. Gesualdo, HMA, I, 552; Gallardo, *Juan Pedro Esnaola*, p. 96; Williams, *Antología*, pp. 92–93.

72. Gesualdo, HMA, I, 555; Gallardo, *Juan Pedro Esnaola*, p. 97; Williams, *Antología*, pp. 95–97.
73. Williams, *Antología*, pp. 96–97.
74. Gesualdo, HMA, I, 486.
75. Ibid., I, 488.
76. Ibid., I, 486, 552, 563.
77. Ibid., I, 483, 555; Gallardo, *Juan Pedro Esnaola*, p. 97.
78. Gesualdo, HMA, I, 564; Gallardo, *Juan Pedro Esnaola*, p. 98.
79. Gesualdo, HMA, I 486, 553.
80. Félix Weinberg, "Contribución a la bibliografía de Esteban Echeverría," in *Universidad*, 45 (1960), 213.
81. Isidoro Montiel, "Ossián en la literatura argentina," in IARB, 19 (1969), 157–162. See Arrieta, "Esteban Echeverría y el Romanticismo en el Plata," II, 32. No support is given for the belief that Echeverría was dependent on Cesarotti's translation of the pseudo-Ossian works.
82. Edgard C. Knowlton, Jr., "Echeverría, traductor de un fragmento del 'Fausto' de Goethe," BAAL, 40 (1975), 317–323.

Chapter Five

1. Battistessa, *La cautiva*, *El matadero*, p. 206; there is a photograph of the statue in figure 44.
2. Carlos Alberto Erro, in prologue, Esteban Echeverría, *Dogma socialista*, Buenos Aires, 1958, p. 11.
3. Palcos, *Dogma socialista*, prologue, pp. vii–xcvi.
4. Ibid., pp. xxxvi–xxxvii.
5. Ibid., pp. xxxix–xl.
6. Ibid., pp. xl–xli.
7. Ibid., p. xlii.
8. Ibid., p. xlviii.
9. Ibid., pp. xlix–l.
10. Ibid., p. liii.
11. Ibid., pp. liv–lv.
12. Ibid., p. lv.
13. Noreen F. Stack, "Peronism," in Helen Delpar, *Enclopedia of Latin America*, New York, etc., 1974, p. 469.
14. Palcos, *Dogma socialista*, prologue, p. lvi.
15. *Constitution of Argentina*, 1853. (as amended), Washington, D.C., 1968, p. 5
16. Palcos, *Dogma socialista*, prologue, p.lix
17. Ibid., p. lxi.
18. Ibid., p. lxi.
19. Ibid., p. lxii.
20. Ibid., p. lxiv.

21. Ibid., pp. lxiv–lxv.
22. Echeverría, OC, Buenos Aires, 1951, pp. 271–274.
23. Jitrik, *Esteban Echeverría*, p. 47.
24. Luis Bernardo Pozzolo, "Personalidad de Esteban Echeverría," in *Diario de Sesiones de la Cámara de Representantes*, Montevideo, No. 1772, Tomo 614, 25 April 1973, p. 282.
25. Ibid., p. 282.
26. Ibid., p. 282.
27. Sara Jaroslavsky Lowy, "Echeverría, Gutiérrez, Alberdi and Sarmiento: Their Reaction to Spain and the Problem of the Language," Diss. Columbia 1970, pp. 10–30.
28. Ibid., p. 157.
29. A. Werner, tr., *Autobiography of Giuseppe Garibaldi*, London, 1889, I, 191.
30. Ibid., I, 226–236.
31. Ibid., I, 230–235.
32. Thomas Moore, *Lalla Rookh*, New York, Boston, 1892, p. 25.
33. Ibid., p. 25.
34. Kittredge, *Sixteen Plays*, p. 533. *I Henry IV*, III,iii, 29–37.
35. Buenaventura Carlos Aribau, *Obras de Miguel de Cervantes Saavedra*, in BAE, Madrid, 1944, I, 271. *Don Quijote*, I, viii.

Chapter Six

1. Mariano Morínigo, "Realidad y ficción de 'El Matadero,' " in *Humanitas*, (Facultad de Filosofía y Letras, Universidad Nacional de Tucumán), 13 (1965) 283–318.
2. Ibid., 283.
3. Ibid., 284.
4. Ibid., 285–286.
5. Ibid., 303–304.
6. Ibid., 306.
7. Ibid., 318.
8. B. Velasco Bayón, ed. P. Antonio Vázquez de Espinosa, *Compendio y descripción de las Indias occidentales*, Madrid, 1969, CCXXXI, 10.
9. Battistessa, *La cautiva*, *El matadero*, p. lxv.
10. See Constance García-Barrios, "The Black in Literature About the Rosas Era," *Revista/Review Interamericana*, 10 (1982), pp. 476–487, and Saúl Sosnowski, "Esteban Echeverría: el intelectual ante la formación del estado," RI, 47: 114–15 (1981), pp. 293–300.
11. David William Foster, "Paschal Symbology in Echeverría's 'El Matadero,' " SSF, 7 (1970), 257–263.
12. Ibid., 258–259.
13. Ibid., 260.

14. Ibid., 263.
15. Matthew 27 : 34.
16. Pier Luigi Crovetto, "Strutture narrative e segni in *El matadero* di E. Echeverría," in *Strumenti critici; rivista quadrimestrale di cultura e critica letteraria*, ll (1977), 292.
17. Ibid., 302.
18. Maria José de Queiroz, "*El Matadero*, pieza en tres actos," in RI, 33 (1967), 105–113.
19. Ibid., 110–112.
20. Ibid., 112.
21. Ibid., 113.
22. C. Enrique Pupo-Walker, "Apuntes sobre la originalidad artística de *El Matadero*, de Esteban Echeverría," in REH, 3 (1969), 204.
23. Ibid., p. 205.
24. Juan Carlos Ghiano, *"El Matadero" de Echeverría y el costumbrismo*, Buenos Aires, 1968.
25. José R. Lomba y Pedraja, ed. Mariano José de Larra, *Artículos políticos y sociales*. Madrid, 1972, p. 130, from "El Hombre-Globo," first published in the *Revista española*, 9 May 1835.
26. Daniel R. Reedy and Joseph R. Jones, ed. *Narraciones ejemplares de Hispanoamérica*, Englewood Cliffs, 1967, pp. 9–31.
27. Emir Rodríguez Monegal, *The Borzoi Anthology of Latin American Literature*, New York, 1977, I, 209–222; Angel Flores, tr. *El matadero*, New York, 1959, a bilingual edition.
28. Fleur Cowles, *Bloody Precedent*, New York, 1952, pp. 89–97.

Chapter Seven

1. Giusti, *Prosa literaria*, p. xxiii.
2. Ibid., pp. xvii-xx. See Marguerite C. Suárez-Murias, "The Influence of Victor Hugo on Esteban Echeverría's Ideology," in LALR, ll (1977), 13.

Chapter Eight

1. David Y. Comstock, ed. *Virgil's Aeneid*, Boston, New York, Chicago, 1896, p. 196. Aeneid, VI, 884, epigraph to Echeverría's "El túmulo de un joven" ("The tumulus of a young man") (III, 457–461)
2. Urien, *Esteban Echeverría*, p. 27.
3. Henríquez Ureña, *Literary Currents*, p. 245.
4. Luis Monguió, "El concepto de poesía en algunos poetas hispanoamericanos representativos," in RHM, 23 (1957), 113–116.

5. Coester, *Literary History*, pp. 148–149.
6. Arturo Capdevila, ed. Rafael Obligado, *Poesías*, Buenos Aires, 1941, pp. 24–29.
7. Ibid., pp. 120–130. Brian and María appear on page 125.
8. Azorín, OC, VII, 1211–1216.
9. Manuel Gálvez, *Bajo la garra anglofrancesa*, Buenos Aires, etc., 1952, p. 199.
10. Gustavo Gabriel Levene, *El mañana: escenificación del romance de Esteban Echeverría y Mariquita Sánchez: pieza en tres actos*, Buenos Aires, c. 1975.
11. Wright and Nekhom, HDA, p. 259.

SELECTED BIBLIOGRAPHY

PRIMARY SOURCES

The Writings of Esteban Echeverría

Publications in book form are listed; some unusually long titles are shortened, and various modern textbook editions are not listed, despite their usefulness and good quality.

1. Collections
Obras completas, ed. Carlos Casavalle (Buenos Aires: Librería de Mayo, 1870–1874) in five volumes, with biography and notes by Juan María Gutiérrez.
Obras completas (Buenos Aires: Zamora, 1951).

2. Editions that mix genres.
La cautiva. El matadero. (Buenos Aires: Peuser, 1946, 1958) Includes annotation and texts established by Angel J. Battistessa.
La cautiva. El matadero. (Buenos Aires: Claridad, 1946) with a prologue by Augusto Raúl Cortázar.

3. Poetry
Avellaneda (Montevideo: Imprenta Francesa, 1850.
La cautiva (Buenos Aires: Imprenta del Siglo, 1864).
La cautiva (Buenos Aires: Emecé, 1966) with sketches by Mauricio Rugendas.
Los consuelos (Buenos Aires: Imprenta Argentina, 1834).
Los consuelos (Buenos Aires: Imprenta Argentina, 1842).
Elvira o La novia del Plata (Buenos Aires: Imprenta Argentina, 1832).
La guitarra (Paris, 1849).
Insurrección del Sud (Montevideo: Imprenta del Comercio del Plata, 1849).
Insurrección del Sud (Buenos Aires: Imprenta Constitución, 1854).
Rimas (Buenos Aires: Imprenta Argentina, 1837).
Rimas (Cádiz: Imprenta de la Viuda de Comes, 1839).
Rimas (Buenos Aires: Imprenta de D. José Arzac, 1846).

4. Literary prose
El matadero (Buenos Aires: Instituto de Literatura Argentina, 1926, 1944) ed. Jorge Max Rohde. A critical edition.
El matadero (New York: Las Américas Publishing Co., 1959) ed. Angel Flores. Text in Spanish and in English.
Prosa literaria (Buenos Aires: Estrada, 1944, 1955) ed. Roberto F. Giusti.

5. Non-literary prose
Cartas a Don Pedro de Angelis (Montevideo: Imprenta del 18 de
    Julio, 1847).
Dogma socialista (Montevideo: Imprenta del Nacional, 1846).
Dogma socialista (Buenos Aires: Imprenta de la Nueva Epoca, 1852).
Dogma socialista (La Plata: Universidad Nacional, 1940) critical
    edition by Alberto Palcos.
Manual de enseñanza moral (Montevideo: Imprenta de la Caridad, 1846).
Manual de enseñanza moral (San Francisco: The History Company, 1892).
Mayo y la enseñanza popular en el Plata (Montevideo: Imprenta del
    Nacional, 1845).

6. Translations into English
The Captive Woman, tr. by Charles W. Humphreys (Buenos Aires:
    R. Grant and Company, 1905).
The Slaughter House, tr. by Angel Flores, see second item under
    4. Literary Prose.

SECONDARY SOURCES

1. Bibliographies
There are two bibliographies devoted to Echeverría: Natalio Kisner-
man's *Contribución a la bibliografía de Esteban Echeverría, 1805–1955*
(Buenos Aires: Universidad Nacional de Buenos Aires, Facultad de Filosofía
y Letras, Instituto de Literatura Argentina "Ricardo Rojas," 1960 and Félix
Weinberg's "Contribución a la bibliografía de Esteban Echeverría" in *Universidad* (Universidad Nacional del Litoral, Santa Fe, Argentina) no. 45
(1960), 159–226.

For more recent titles, reference should be made to annual listings in
the *Year's Work in Modern Language Studies*, the *Handbook of Latin American Studies*, and the *Publications of the Modern Language Association*, as
well as sections on Echeverría in David William Foster:*Argentine Literature,
A Research Guide, 2nd ed., rev. and expanded* (New York and London:
Garland Publishing, Inc., 1982) and Angel Flores: *Bibliografía de escritores
hispanoamericanos* (New York: Gordian Press, 1975).

2. Books, parts of books, and articles
ARRIETA, RAFAEL ALBERTO, "Esteban Echeverría y el Romanticismo
    en el Plata," in *Historia de la literatura argentina* (Buenos
    Aires: Peuser, 1958), II, 19–113. A comprehensive survey,
    by a firsthand researcher, strong on literary relations.

BORELLO, RODOLFO A., "Notas a la Cautiva," in *Logos* (Universidad
    de Buenos Aires), 13–14 (1977–78), 69–84. Interesting for
    its analysis of "Cartas a un amigo" as a probable source,
    and other insights into "The Captive Woman."

GARCÍA MÉROU, MARTÍN, *Ensayo sobre Echeverría* (Buenos Aires: Jackson, 1944). Reprint of one of the most solid studies on Echeverría's works viewed in context, originally published in 1894.

LAMARQUE, NYDIA, *Echeverría el poeta* (Buenos Aires: 1951). Undoubtedly the most sensitive and appreciative study of Echeverría's verse, and the relationship between it and the man himself.

LANUZA, JOSÉ LUIS, *Esteban Echeverría y sus amigos* (Buenos Aires: Raigal, 1951). A lively and trustworthy account of Echeverría's milieu, friends, and life.

MORALES, ERNESTO, *Esteban Echeverría* (Buenos Aires: Claridad, 1950). A readable, illustrated account of the man and his works; perhaps the best balanced mixture of background and biography, with attention to all the works.

ORTIZ, RICARDO M., *El pensamiento económico de Echeverría, trayectoria y actualidad* (Buenos Aires: Raigal, 1953). A sympathetic study emphasizing the practicality of Echeverría's economic views.

PALACIOS, ALFREDO LORENZO, *Estevan Echeverría, albacea del pensamiento de Mayo* (Buenos Aires: Claridad, 1951). A thorough, well-documented work concentrating on the historical and political backgrounds.

PALCOS, ALBERTO, *Historia de Echeverría* (Buenos Aires: Emecé, 1960). A basic modern study, rich in documentation, especially in correspondence and recent discoveries.

POPESCU, ORESTE, *El pensamiento social y económico de Echeverría* (Buenos Aires: Editorial Americana, 1954). An excellent orientation for the study of the poet's social and economic ideas.

PUPO-WALKER, ENRIQUE, "Originalidad y composición de un texto romántico: 'El matadero', de Esteban Echeverría," in his *El cuento hispanoamericano ante la crítica* (Madrid: Editorial Castalia, 1973), pp. 37–49. Revised version of a useful article for the genre of *The Slaughterhouse*, referred to in Notes and References.

ROJAS, RICARDO, *Historia de la literatura argentina* (Buenos Aires: Kraft, 1957). A standard and comprehensive view divided between Volumes II, 463–479 and V, 155–237.

SCARI, ROBERT M., "The Esthetic Ideas of Echeverría and Aspects of Romanticism in *El Matadero*," *Iberoromania*, 16 (1982): 38–53. Of particular interest for literary history and esthetics.

SUÁREZ-MURIAS, MARGUERITE C., "The Influence of Victor Hugo on Esteban Echeverría's Ideology," *Latin American Literary Review*, ll (1977), 13–21. Emphasizes the Paris stay and the impact of Hugo's prefaces on the poet's thought.

URIEN, CARLOS MARÍA, *Esteban Echeverría. Ensayo crítico-histórico sobre su vida y obras, con motivo de la erección de su estatua* (Buenos Aires: Cabaut, 1905). Of interest both for its comprehensive treatment of the life and works and its evaluation of Echeverría one hundred years after his birth.

WILLIAMS ALZAGA, ENRIQUE, *La pampa en la novela argentina* (Buenos Aires: Estrada, 1955). Despite the appearance of the word *novela*, "novel," in the title, this work on the pampa-inspired literature is interesting for its comments on "The Captive Woman" and "The Slaughterhouse."

Note: In this brief listing of books, parts of books, and articles an attempt is made to give a sampling of useful items, few of which have been directly referred to in the Notes and References. As a whole they provide some initial guidance to general works in which Echeverría is treated in some detail (e.g. Rojas), works that emphasize some aspect or facet (e.g. Ortiz), or that present in readable form a comprehensive survey (e.g. Morales). They are by no means the only, or even the best of such works necessarily; they are meant to be varied, not exclusive.

INDEX

118

119